# Journeys of Recovery
# Poetic Expressions

Donette A. DaCosta

Lisa Nicole Publishing
Lisanicolealexander.com
Gotha, FL 34734
Printed in the United States of America
ISBN: 978-1-7375515-2-2

# DEDICATION

This book of prose and poems is dedicated to all the amazing women that God has placed in my life and also to my family. Your continuous prayers and encouragement have propelled me to LIVE. To you all, I say, "I L -O-V-E you!"

## About the Author

The author is an Educator who holds a bachelor's degree in Educational Administration and a diploma in Early Childhood Education, respectively. She studied at the University of the West Indies and Shortwood Teachers' College in Jamaica and is presently the Principal of an Early Childhood Development Centre in Jamaica. She is also a part-time instructor at H.E.A.R.T TRUST/NTA Garmex Academy, where she teaches Early Childhood Education.

Donette resides in the beautiful tropical island of Jamaica, where the people are warm and friendly. She is a divorcee with two amazing adults. Donette travels to the United States quite often to spend time with her family. The family is closely knit, enjoys spending time, and having fun together. Among the things she enjoys doing are traveling, playing a good game of scrabble or dominoes, and cooking. She loves going to the beach, as well as relaxing and enjoying the sand, sun, and sea.

Donette enjoys working with children and boasts that her job allows her to do just that. The author attends "Church on the Rock" in Kingston, Jamaica, where she is an avid worshipper and teaches Sunday school; Donette is rewarded by seeing the transformation in the lives of the teens that she teaches, week after week. Being able to praise and worship the Lord are the most fulfilling parts of her spiritual life. She affirms that God has given her many second chances, and that is why she is happy when she is given a chance to speak and represent him.

# ACKNOWLEDGMENT

Writing a book about my life is a surreal process, harder than I thought yet more rewarding than I could have ever imagined.

None of this would have been possible without all the amazing people that God has placed in my life.

First and foremost, I would like to give thanks to my Lord and Savior Jesus Christ for entrusting to me these EXPERIENCES to impart to His people.

To my daughter – Hanna-Joye, and my son Donelle, for their willingness to allow me to fulfill my God-given purpose in life.

To my parents Arthur and Dorothy, for all the sacrifices they have made to help their children to become who we are today and for all the fervent prayers they prayed for us.

To my sisters, Gayann, Zonnette, Sharnette, and Francia, you have been a tower of support and encouragement throughout my entire journey.

To my brother Garnette, you prayed, you fasted, and God did the rest.

To my brothers-in-law in-law Michael and Charles, you have demonstrated that there are still godly men who absolutely love and adore their wives.

To my only niece JayAnna, you continuously remind me that God still answers prayers.

To my nephews, Jathan, Jaden, Jahven, and Jayce, you are my daily inspirations.

To my mentor Dr. Stennett, your words of wisdom have been a tower of strength to me.

To Christine, Audrey, Dionne, my dearest friends, for believing in me and seeing this project through fruition.

To Aunt Del, you are my inspiration.

My family you all supported me and were there with me throughout the journey.

To my publishing team, thank you for working with me in making this book, my dream, a reality.

# PREFACE

In 2020 I published my first book, and oh, what an amazing journey this has been. I am thankful for every opportunity I get to share my journey with people from all over the world. Since the publication of my book, I have had hundreds of women who have called or have written to share their stories. Some stories are joyful, while others are painful and sad. People all over the world go through different types of abuse, hurt, pain, frustration, and trauma. It is real. Christ provides us with Hope, and there are avenues that are there to provide help for everyone. I have had so many people saying thank you for writing and sharing your story. My story is my truth, and I continue to share this with the world.

Since the publication of my book, I have been given a platform to speak and to share my journey, of which I am so thankful. I have spoken at Women's Conferences in Jamaica and Canada. I have done several virtual speaking engagements with people in different churches and groups. I will continue to use my voice and my writings. These are the tools that God has given to me to make a difference in our world.

# TABLE OF CONTENTS

# INTRODUCTION

These poems are pieces of writing that were carefully written to express the writer's heart and journey through different stages of her life. The choice of words and expression used speaks to the writer's Caribbean culture and her religious belief as a Christian. Each poem speaks to her own experiences and her journey. She strongly believes in the power of love and forgiveness, as this is expressed in several of her poems.

The words chosen express the beauty of words and the sound words can make when they are carefully arranged, often in short lines which rhyme. The author's emotions played a pivotal part in her writing. Her moments of extreme and insuppressible emotions and thoughts brought a sense of catharsis within her, something she hopes the readers will find from each poem.

The author started writing poems after her separation from a marriage of eighteen years. This was an avenue that she felt free to express how she felt without being judged by everyone.
The author shares poems that may put the readers in a melancholy mood, joyful, happy, and thankful mood, while others might inspire and uplift.

It is the author's hope that these poems will bring a new awareness to people's life, restoration of faith and marriages, and that the readers will find solace in the times of adversities and strength for new beginnings and new seasons. The author hopes that this anthology of poems will evoke self-introspection while inducing a hurricane of emotions in each reader while pushing them to get a better understanding of themselves.

The author concludes that writing these poems has taught her that the best part about writing poetry is that there is no "right" or "best" kind of poetry. It is that which tugs at the heartstrings of each reader that will be most beneficial. Poetry is a beautiful and powerful combination of words that in just a few sentences can speak volumes. When speech doesn't help, poetry does.

# LOVE

*This love is real. It goes very deep. It's unconditional, an intense feeling of deep affection that you feel for that special someone.*

# HOW COULD YOU ?

Way down, very deep in my heart

It hurts

Relieved and happy that I am free from all your hurt.

Sometimes I still feel angry.

Why am I the one left with no one by my side?

Scares left that are constant reminders of a life I once lived with

someone I loved.

Though not visual for you to see.

My stomach tightens, and my heart races

Still trying to understand how could you?

What could I have done to deserve all this pain?

Yes, in my heart, I know my love for you has slowly diminished

After so many years.

# LORD, I WILL WAIT

Lord, I will wait

Beneath the pain, reality stares

Right in my very eyes, loneliness and the absence of intimacy

Despite this reality, I still try to find the things that will quell this

loneliness inside

Oftentimes finding options to satisfy

Numerous questions with very few answers

Many make suggestions and give advice

I wish this were like a job you advertise

Then interview after you have shortlisted the desired

The search continues, but the results seem futile.

Frustrated, I have become

Vowed never to settle for anything less than God's very best

By now, I should have learned not to trust my feelings only my heart

The pain gets intense; I cannot hide

The sexual urges arise, and the need for companionship just can't

subside

When will I, if ever find that love I so desire?

I have been trying to use work and so many other things to drown my

thoughts

After a while, I realize

This just works for only a few hours

After which I feel like a sinking ship

Loneliness is real; I cannot lie

But I must continue to stand my ground.

I am God's very best, this I have known

As I reflect, I must admit, I try to fight those thoughts that bombard

my mind

While constantly feeling defeated with little or no success at times

I will continue to try as I will not compromise

I turn to the one who wrote my book

And who knew me from the very first look

God, you have my life in your hands

I look to you because you are the only one who really understands my

heart

Yes, you know exactly what I want

And so Lord, I have decided to stop helping you in this process

Lord, I surrender everything to you

And one more thing Lord, I have decided that as of today

I will wait, yes Lord, I will wait

Hard as it is, I will wait

I know you have that special person, and I know he will also meet me

In time, yes Lord, the right time

And so, I will wait regardless of the pain.

I will wait on my right time.

# HEART ACHES

Oh, how my heartaches

For the love I so deserve

I have spent my life giving, sharing, and loving

Lord, I really want you to find that one that will love me regardless of

and will wait for me.


And so I will wait

Material things I have achieved

I refuse to be naive

I am proud of where I am,

I am proud of who I have become

I am proud of where you, God, have taken me from

And so I will wait.


The test of faith is real

Life sometimes becomes surreal

As I wait, the wait seems endless

Reminded by your word

Lord, I clearly understand

You don't need my help

I let go, I surrender

And I will wait

Loneliness is real, the need for love, companionship, and intimacy

The need for sex, yes real fulfilling sex

The need to be held and reassured

Why do I pretend this is not so?

Why do I have to hide these feelings with facades of lies?

Why do I have to pretend that I am ok when I'm not

All this must stop

And so Lord, I will wait.

# FEELINGS I CAN'T HIDE

Why do I feel this way?

Why do I want to hear your voice as soon as I am awake?

I spend my day thinking and praying that you are ok.

Why do I want to end my day just talking and laughing with you?

You are so easy to talk to.

Your childlike antics surely teaches me not to take life so seriously,

Our upbringing and experiences in life certainly make us who we are-

Different but Unique.

Personality and heart are so much more important than what the

naked eye perceives,

No wonder God says, He looks at the inward parts

Trust me, He never lies.

The outward parts can become tricky and misleading,

so I have learned to trust my heart,

Trust regardless of.


As I go through each day, I am amazed at how close we have become.

I guess that's what true friendship is about.

And the truth is, I look forward to hearing you say

"don't worry, you will be ok."

Yes, Lord! I know according to your Word; this too shall pass.

I know in time I will be ok.

For only God knows what lies ahead,

And so in spite of-

I am learning each day to trust His heart and His hand.

# EMOTIONAL ROLLER COASTER

Today my emotions went on a roller coaster ride,

This feeling of loneliness I cannot hide,

My tears I did not try to dry.

Why me, why not me?

How long, why so much pain?

So many questions raced through my mind,

For a moment, my thoughts bombarded my mind,

Tears rolled down my cheeks as I ask God, why?


I felt as though I was stuck on pause

And prayed that when play was pressed,

All these feelings would be gone.

I rehearsed the scriptures in my mind and hummed some of my

favorite tunes,

I tried so hard to concentrate but, reality stared me right in the face.

This loneliness is real; I cannot hide it.

I must keep my mind busy, so my thoughts can subside

I must capture the truth, though the wait may be long,

There is a joy that comes in the morning.

I must remain focused,

The best is yet to come,

I must not allow my emotions to drown me, not at this time.

I must stand fast and declare the truth,

I must be patient and work on me.

I will not settle for mediocrity,

I know I deserve the very best.

I am a strong, beautiful black woman,

I must continue to hold my head high,

I know I will be just fine.

# DONETTE, THAT'S ME

D- dandy, a description of you!

O – outlook, pleasing to all.

N – name, a pleasant one indeed.

E -elate, you make others happy.

T- talent, hidden or not.

T -tried, tried, and true you.

E -enjoy, your life can be fun!

Donette is my name, and I am not ashamed.

For in my name lies an abundance of possibilities and potentials,

That will continue to materialize over time.

Myriads of blessings I have received,

Donette will continue to aim high and reach for the sky.

In my name, DONETTE, greatness lies.

# DAMN YOU

Damn you

The pain and anger I now feel

Numbs my very being

How could you hurt me so much?

And then pretend I am to blame

You walk around with no remorse

Never one-day expressing regret

Your words and action have inflicted scars

Too deep for many to see

Leaving wounds, only God can heal

Yes, I once loved you with all my heart

But your actions certainly caused distrust

If only you knew how much I cared

You would not have defied my trust

# WHAT IS LOVE ?

Is love an illusion,

A fantasy or a dream,

Am I delusional?


Is the word love just a mere utterance?

Of your selfishness and greed,

That you casually echo

In an effort to get your own desire.


How can you say this is love?

When to me, there is no demonstration of kindness,

No closeness, no togetherness.

Frustrated with your cold and callous remarks,

As tears of hurt and pain wash my face.

Longing for reassurance of your love,

The words from your lips were like coals of fire,

Destroying the little confidence I had left.

Forgive me if I am wrong,

But, if this is love, I must be mad!

Love for me is an act of doing,

Showing appreciation.

Ensuring that the fire is kept alive by simply

Supporting and treasuring the bonds of love.

It is now clear to me that your love was a mere illusion.

# AGONIZING PAIN

Broken Promises

Crushed Hopes

Unpleasant Memories

Shattered Dreams

Destined Fate

Excruciating Pains

A Wounded Heart

Agonizing Moments

Uncertain Future

Shaken Faith

Obliterated Memories

Aborted Goals

Unresolved yet

Determined to STAND

# LOVE DISGUISED

The pain I feel is best described

With words, I just cannot hide

Countless moments of conflict

Crippling this very heart of mine

Confrontations, too many to be disguised

Praying someday this will all subside

Emotions, crushed from every side

Complexities of my life

Are too many to hide

Your callous remarks

Were cold as ice

They froze my very core

After a while, they became chronic

My love for you was compromised

How could you expect me

To be caring, compassionate, and content?

After all our lives, you were just a great pretense.

# FORGIVENESS

*It is the action or process of forgiving or being forgiven. It is a conscious, deliberate decision to release feelings of resentment or vengeance toward a person who has harmed you, regardless of whether they deserve your forgiveness. It does not mean forgetting, nor does it mean condoning or excusing the offenses.*

# DETERMINED TO STAND

Broken, wounded

Determined to live,

Regardless of the pain

I try so hard to hide,

Dreams are shattered at every side

Anger, rage

How can I overcome this pain?

Thoughts of resentment race through my mind

What action should I take? I want him to pay

He has taken all my youthful years away

Tears of hurt and anger roll down my cheeks

My heart feels hard; I must let go

I must begin to forgive

I must leave everything to the King

I must not allow him to WIN

Determined, I am going to live

Time heals, isn't that what they say?

Or should I say, love, takes time to heal?

Despite the pain one feels, what am I to believe?

When my heart aches from all this pain,

And the agonizing moments of truth hit like bullets,

I must set myself free just like the dove,

Who searches for its love,

I must let go of these dreadful woes,

Tainted by unhappiness, time heals, time will heal

Let it remove the anguish and shame,

Caused by years of selfishness and mistrust

I must allow time to heal so that I can be free

From painful memories

And with time,

I will learn to live a life full of happiness, love, and trust.

Love takes time to heal

# CLOSED DOOR

I told myself I would never let anyone get close to my heart again

That door will remain closed

My past experiences have taught me some valuable lessons

About life and these people called men

I know I am vulnerable,

Praying that my past I will never relive

And then you came along,

The pain I felt slowly recedes

I am smiling, determined to win,

The more we talk is the closer I feel

The longing each day for your warm embrace,

Your tender and passionate touch.

I want to hold you, hug you, and squeeze you

While placing my ear on your chest just to listen to your heartbeat

The countdown of meeting you has already started

It seems like forever but, I am constantly reminded,

All good things come to those who wait.

And so, I patiently await that great moment!

We will see each other

And the truth will be known.

# CANVAS COLOURS

My life, my story, its authenticity belongs to me

My life, my canvas created with various hues

Tones beautifully crafted from my birth

Dependent on the dominance of life

Blended and mixed, creating a kaleidoscope of colours

My story unfolds as I live and breathe on this earth

Yet independent of intensity or lightness that which we sometimes
take for granted

Determined to display characteristics that were inherited

Some so dark, I pray no one sees

Don't criticize my canvas because you don't know the intensity of its
brush strokes

I love my colourful canvas, especially the lines invisible to the naked
eye

The great artist of all times continues to add to my mural, my canvas,
my life

The beauty some will never see or fail to appreciate

They have not the perspective of my Creator

My canvas has His signature

As He clearly stated in His word, Genesis 1 verse 27

I know without a shadow of a doubt

The hues on my canvas are engraved by His truth

I was carefully chosen; I am unique

I am fearfully and wonderfully made

I must retain my authenticity

I must walk in my God-given purpose.

I must allow the master to continue to apply His brush

His strokes I cannot touch

I am divinely positioned for the glory of God

That His glory can be seen in and through me as His masterpiece

And while you view His aesthetic creation

Please remember He is not yet done; I am still undergoing

construction.

A tweak here and another brush stroke there

My canvas, my life.

# WHAT IS LIFE AFTER DIVORCE ?

Life after Divorce

You asked- what is it like?

For me, it means so many different things

Its freedom from my past, freedom from pretense

Its freedom from all the pain inflicted from years of trauma


Initiated by this demon of abuse

It is gratifying to know I am no longer bound

It is hope that reassures, knowing all I need, and desire comes from

God

I am not walking alone though without a husband; He is my comfort


It's a reality check, removal of years of facade, becoming new and real

Facing all my fears and learning new ways of how to deal with them,

Welcoming true happiness that comes from within.

Embracing every feeling that constantly assures me that yes I can,

I will be okay

Its freedom knowing I can do anything I want to do on any given day,

That sometimes means sitting and gazing in the sun or basking in the

rain.

I have learned to smile at my own jokes

I wear a smile instead of a frown.

I see the beauty in people and all of God's creation,

I cherish every moment I get to be with myself

It is waking up and not feeling accountable to man, only to God


There are days when I do get a little emotional,

Sad about my past but happily embrace my future

My days are filled with sunshine and blessings from above,

I'm thankful for buddies who have my back and constantly remind

me of how special I am.

Family that goes above and beyond to ensure that I never walk alone.

I understand all this to be God's, unmerited love,

Life after Divorce is awesome! I am discovering something new each

day.

I am embracing.

I am loving me.


I am truly learning about me,

There is so much joy in the beauty that I see around each day,

I have learned to cherish silence and to listen to God's voice,

It's in the quietness that He speaks, and so I take every opportunity to

listen.

I pen my thoughts to paper and find it quite therapeutic.

I use my time wisely, as I now understand what King Solomon says

A man's gift makes room for him and brings him before great men.

My divorce has helped me to be more focused, appreciative,

I see God's grace in everything, and I am happy; I am free.

Some days I feel like a bird, as free as can be,

As beautiful as diamonds, rubies, and pearls.

Life after divorce has been rewarding and fulfilling for me,

It's a new beginning; it's a new journey.

I embrace it with all my energy.

It's a road not many get to travel,

I am privileged to have traveled both.

Life after divorce is just awesome!

# DEDICATION

You knew me before I was formed.

you knew my life from start to end.

You intricately designed my every step, Godly parents I will never forget.

Three sisters, three brothers I cared for with no regrets,

Our love for each other guided our thoughts,

This love can never be bought.

A home of love we created -a bond so strong no one could break.

I cherish those precious days that laughter filled our atmosphere

A bond we deemed great, inseparable then and still is today.

Living together, just us teenagers was never easy,

We solved our problems and resolved our conflicts.

Teeth and tongue sometimes clashed.

Belt and thump left hurtful scars, lessons learned,

Obedience is key

Respect your elders one and all

Too young to sometimes disagree,

We did our best to prove them wrong

Together we walked with heads held high,

My siblings, I love dearly to this day.

Our childhood memories are forever etched in our hearts,

These we embrace as we continue this journey called LIFE.

# MIGRATION

September 1988 was the year you took the step of faith

You wanted a better life for yourself and your family

At 15 years old, I knew our lives would never be the same

As the eldest child, I consoled myself with the thought

That one day we all would take the shiny aircraft

You left very early in the morning,

I could see the tears in your eyes,

This would be the last day you see your children's faces for a while

Two days after you left, it rained nonstop

Before we knew it, the island had a storm

Yes, Gilbert, one we would never forget

And so the rains poured, there was no power, and the roof was lifted;

We were all exposed to the elements. So thankful for good neighbors,

we got a place to rest our heads.

The hardest part of it, we were missing our mom, yet we worked assiduously to clean up the debris.

Everything changed in just mere seconds,

Grateful to God and good neighbors,

We overcame this dreadful storm.

It was not the least an easy one, but faith told us to carry on.

Together we held hands, determined to stay strong,

with our father's help, a new life began.

Together we must carry on, so I quickly took on the mantle,

to care for my younger ones.

I was the sister, who went to every meeting,

my shoulders, they cried on.

I was the one to wipe their nose and gave the hugs just to reassure.

Hard as it was, I held the course; I must be strong for each one.

And while we understood, our hearts ached for the love only a mother can give

Though dad tried, it was not the same.

And so for us migration meant to separate, we waited for many years until 1996

When mom returned to our happy home, her kids were all grown.

Tears of joy rolled down our cheeks,

Thankful to God for this memorable day.

Migration is filled with mixed emotions.

It's a journey only for the strong.

Even though many things have changed,

We are thankful to God for keeping us all together.

# COURTSHIP

Who would have ever thought that you and I would be one?

How we watched each other from a distance, admiring our every move.

What struck me the most was your breathtaking smile and that sexy walk,

Your outstanding musical ability was noticeable by all, including me.

Each time I saw you, there was the flutter of butterflies in my stomach, yet we managed to disguise it.

On those long romantic walks, so many questions you would ask, while the answers I was not afraid to hide.

Hands held close, sweet kisses on our lips, strokes through my hair as we expressed our love and embraced.

This feeling, though, was hard to hide; we believe our faith brought us this fate.

We continued to pray and trusted our faith as we continued our date.

Two hearts, they say, beat as one

this was so as we held each other's hand.

To be in this courtship was the best; our prayers were always- God, please do the rest.

We loved each other; we became the inseparable two.

Many watchful eyes open to see how long it would have lasted.

Lasted it did, our courtship never ended but continued into what we anticipated-

Two hearts forever beating as one.

# YES, I CHANGED

Stumbled upon some old emails you sent me from 2012

From reading them, it was quite noticeable that we had so many

problems in our marriage, too numerous to name

Oh, how I prayed that as the head of our home,

You would have made more effort to get the professional help we

needed.

Many suggestions were made, yet you ignored them all

You verbally said you didn't need their help

I didn't agree, but left it to you,

As I worked on me

Oh my goodness! We have been playing the blame game for years

You really had no idea how much I loved and adored you

My kindness was often mistaken for selfishness,

I tried so hard for you to notice

But you didn't

You expected so much of me, and I tried my best

But never felt my best was good enough.

It was quite easy for you to ignore this, as your eyes and heart were

someplace else

I tried to understand why your interest in work was skewed,

You lacked the tenacity and drive to go the extra mile for your family

Why were the financial responsibilities always mine?

Why was it okay with you for me to take care of you and our children?

I would do everything I could to make my family happy,

But felt no one was there to take care of me


Oh, I cried,

My dream was that you would at least show some of the same interest you showed in your online scrabble and Chess games,

that you and she would play for hours daily

Yet, I would be right there, and you didn't even blink an eye,

Or at least acknowledge my presence

This was noticeable even to our children,

You really think you could continue treating me this way and expect me not to change?


Yes, I changed the moment you told me God told you to keep your friendship with her,

Yes, I changed because she became first, and I was now last.

I changed because I was tired of competing with those girls and church,

Yes, I changed

I needed my husband and not a roommate

Yes, I changed

I needed more than you were willing to give,

Yes, I changed

Because your actions ripped my heart

Yes, I changed

Because I was no longer important to you,

Yes, I changed

Because I no longer loved you.

My love was taken for granted by you when you choose her


How could you?

And then you really expected me to always be there for you?

I tried for years but could no longer continue

It was either her or me

And honestly, I think she should have you


After 18 years of marriage,

After all, I have done,

You still questioned my love and my faithfulness

I am done!

You choose her

Yes, I changed,

Because you changed

# LIFE

On this journey of life

There are many roads that lead to various paths,

Each with a unique layout

Thoroughly designed

Created and crafted just for you

Depending on the path chosen

Your experience can be favorable or unfavorable,

Delightful or melancholy

The master architect intricately designed each path

That will lead you into His plan and destiny

So chose your path carefully,

This journey never ends

# SEASONS

Many people come into our lives at different times and seasons.

People come, people go

Each making their own contribution to one's life

Every experience teaches wisdom,

Indelible marks are imprinted

On the templates of our hearts

Too many for one to understand

So, never take anyone for granted

They are all a part of the master's plan

Treat everyone with love and respect.

These two go a far way

Love people in spite of

Inspire regardless of

Each individual helps to complete every experience in your life

# PAIN

The pain I feel is real. It is the state of feeling broken, wounded, loss of self, disconnection from everyone and everything that matters, its deep sorrow, sadness that often causes depression.

Grief.

Intense distress.

Loneliness.

Isolation.

Sadness

# DID YOU LOVE ME ?

Did you love me?

Did you *really* love me?

Did you really love *me?*

Yes!!! Me

In my mind, these questions linger,

Do you really know what love means?


Love is patient, love is kind, and love is gentle all the time

It is not easily angered

Forgetting all wrongs

Love is caring,

Love is protecting the people and things you hold dear to your heart

Love is a priceless treasure,

One that cannot be bought or sold,

Traded or auctioned

With value far greater than dollars or cents,

This kind of love requires much care- it is just very rare


Was I ever dear to your heart?

Was I the item you promised you would treasure forever?

After all the drama and misguided thoughts

I am confused

If this is love, what is hate?


Love is holding hands through thick and thin,

It's walking in the sunshine and the rain,

It's agreeing to disagree,

It's saying I am sorry, even when you are right

It's providing the support to stand even when knees give way,

From the weight of this thing call pain

It's supporting one's willingness to fight; you know together you are

stronger.

It is believing and reassuring that yes, we can

Regardless of the odds,

Love is the beauty you see in each other's eyes,

Despite the tears or the pain


Love is that little spark, only true lover sees,

If carefully fanned, will overtime blaze

And lights up the entire atmosphere

What was the answer?

Please tell me

Did you ever love me?

# DEMONS OF ABUSE

Demons of abuse

We call you out by name

You lurk around in the dark places of people's lives

You torture and torment the deep things of our very core

You carefully orchestrate your plans

With so many disguises

Your strength is one's emotions and things from their past

You thrive on lies, demons of abuse you can no longer hide

We recognize you with our eyes


Demons of physical abuse

Why do you continue to inflict us with those big blows?

You took our weakness and enforced your strength,

You have no idea we could be freed from you

Demons of verbal abuse, I pretended not to hear you for years

Your sound was deafening. I can no longer hide

How I tried to ignore you

They say sticks and stone can break my bones,

But your words can do me nothing

Lies, lies, your words cut right through my heart

I felt your pain much more than the bruises and wounds you inflicted

For weeks my mind was bombarded by your annoying voice
Traumatized by your negative echoes
Syntax used clearly demonstrated that your ego was compromised
Ignoring you was the last thing you anticipated, and so I did
Even though those words tore my very core
I recognize you, and I boldly say no more

Demons of financial abuse you can no longer hide
I call you out, why do I have to give you an account of every penny I
worked or spent
Your subtle tactics were often manipulating you asked that we
prepared a budget
One that reflected all my income
The truth you had none, well that's what you clearly echoed
Your language was intimidating and quite demanding
Sometimes, I honestly thought this was the norm in every marriage
You demon, I now recognize this
This was the beginning of your trap
I must get out of this

Today I bring exposure to you, demons of abuse
No one should suffer from your terror of humiliation
Your constant put-downs and sarcasm.
My self-esteem slowly eroded
While self-doubt became so paralyzing
This cycle must be broken, and I cannot do it alone

I will not sit back and watch you win

Enough is enough, my self-confidence, I must regain

Today I break my silence. This is the end

I must shine the light on these demons of abuse

I must speak out as I am determined to WIN.

# OPEN HEART

I opened my heart to your love from the day we met,
I decided that I want you to be my forever love.
Not just today, not just for a day,
But all the time and every day.

I vowed to love you 'til death do part,
My heart belongs to you,
You are my dream, my life, my all,
You make me feel so complete.

The tenderness and sweet caress of your lips,
Your kiss is quite inviting,
Who would have thought a kiss would be so magical?
It leaves you in awe, always wanting more.
You pulling me close to you while I rest my head on your chest,
Listening to your heart throbbing against your breastbone.

The feeling of intimacy is so real
Our beliefs get tested every day
We vowed to wait for each other until our wedding day,

These feelings are so hard to resist,

Together we must get past this test.


This love cannot be tainted,

It cannot be hidden,

It is deep and feels like it will last forever.

So time will tell, as you and I hold on to all this magical feeling called

love

# CHURCH DISGUISE

Why does the church continue to pretend that everything is all well?
When will the leaders of the church admit that the reflection of the
world is the reflection of the church?
While the world looks to the church for answers,
Why has the church not taken charge by waging war on the devil?
Taking back everything that the enemy has stolen from the people of
God,
By the blood of Jesus Christ

When will the church remove its blinders and see the true reality?
The church has become a failed organism,
Trying to birth life through its powerlessness
Sometimes one feels like a caterpillar, weaving its web to be free from
The cocoon of hypocrisy, pretense, and sin
Webs woven so thick that it leaves no room for the sweet Holy Spirit
to operate
Not my will Lord but yours be done; this should be our daily anthem.

When will the church stop being fake?
And deal with the issues that are real?

Stop being hypocrites and sugar-coating realities,

Hurting men and hurting women,

Produce hurting families and dysfunctional homes.

The pain inflicted penetrates way too deep

Your words have failed to match your actions,

Too often, you say, do as I say but not as I do,

Seriously, when did you think this was ok?

Jesus Christ, our great example, His actions, and words match.

So why are you not emulating this pattern,

Why do you continue and expect great results?


Men and women whom God has called,

Why do you hide behind the pulpit?

Pretending that you are so faultless?

Filled with deceit and lies,

When will you stop pretending to be perfect when God knows you

not?

When will you make room for Him,

So He can do what He will?

When will the church admit that it has failed?

Repent! So we will all be saved

From the wrath and anger of our God

Which is imminent,

His wrath brings fury; God hates sin.


Men and women of God, those whom God has called

To lead His people out of darkness into light,

Those to whom He has placed His mantle on.

To whom much is given, much is required,

Why do you continue to pretend as if there is no end?

Can't you see the wrongs meted out to those who you lead?

Why have you become men-pleasers?

Why have you become silent?

Why do you use his word at your own convenience?

To cover your innuendos.

When was it ok for you to be sexual predators and molesters?

We confided in you; we needed your counsel,

We open our hearts, yet you played with our vulnerability.

You misrepresented the truth,

You took sides with Satan,

You ruined both of our reputations


The scars you inflicted

Even though not physical,

Left us with wounds no bandage could hide

Embellished by years of trauma inflicted by you,

These I can no longer hide

Fear of you torments my soul; why did you torture us?

We trusted you but, our innocence, you forcefully took

You deserve His wrath; you deserve His judgment!

Turn and repent, we beg of you!

His love He freely gives to everyone, even you.

# GOD'S GIFT TO US~ DONELLE

What a surprise

I was pregnant with my number two

I remembered my prayer years ago

Yes, this time, my heart wanted a boy

There you are you are on your way

I am more and more excited every day

Our lives will be rearranged

Another of God's great blessings

He has given unto us

Everyone was excited, praying you were a boy

Your dad wanted you to carry on his family name

This time I couldn't wait; an ultrasound was scheduled right away

The doctor said, "It's a boy" my heart leaped within

We prayed he was right as we got lots of blue

You were so much like your sister

My belly got bigger, my face fatter

You are a strong little guy - your muscles showed

Our hearts filled with joy as we anxiously await your arrival

Your little sister was super happy

She would rub my tummy and talk to you

She read you stories and sang songs for you; she was super excited.

I knew she would be a great big sister to you, my little bumblebee


Name hunting took a while; it was so hard to decide

So many persons wanted to add their view

And so your Auntie GayAnn decided that she should name you

She came the closest, and I loved her choice

And so she named you Donelle, a boy after moms own heart


Count down began at week thirty-six

I was so heavy I could hardly walk

Week thirty-seven, the doctor said, no more delays

I was filled with so much JOY

You have taught me patience, showed me strength,

and now I was ready for the world to meet you,

my superstar,

And so God answered my prayer again, a boy we had

I promised you everything,

And NOTHING will stand in my way.

God's precious gift, our Donelle.

# GOD'S GIFT TO US- HANNA-JOYE

Before I was even married

I prayed and asked God for you both

My prayer was always to have a sweet girl first and my second a

handsome boy

And so when news came of your conception

Excitement filled our hearts

Didn't want to break the excitement of it all

So I refused to be told your gender

All I wanted was to know you were developing just fine

Anxious moments they were for everyone

As you were going to be the 1st grandbaby for my parents

My stomach was big and round; everyone thought I was having twins

You stretched, you wiggled and moved as you grew stronger each day

There were so many emotions

New thoughts, new fears, and most importantly YOU

Our hearts were filled with joy as we anxiously awaited your grand
arrival

Name selection was really hard

I needed one that was unique and cute

And after searching and researching, we found the perfect two

Month eight, the countdown began

Tick tock, 123, just like the big clock

All was well up to 36 weeks

God decided it was time for us to finally meet

And so with a few challenges,

The doctors raced to save our lives

Everything was happening so fast

All I could do was pray

In my heart asking God, please let this baby be okay

Hours after still medicated, I heard a whisper, and they said it was a
GIRL

We spent days in the hospital; they wanted to ensure you were fine

Disappointment came when I was told I had to leave you behind

You were not well enough to go home

Oh, we prayed and held on to our faith

Trusting God that you would be okay

And yes, He did, after two weeks, I brought you home

Our home was filled with this new happiness and bundle of JOY

We named you Hanna-Joye

A name we all knew you would love

And so God answered my prayer a beautiful girl we had

I promise you everything, and NOTHING will stand in my way.

# A NEW HOPE

It has been raining since yesterday,

It's such a joy to listen to the rain

As it pitter-patter on the roof

Regardless of what is happening in my life, the rain brings such a

calm.


And so I lie in bed clutching onto my pillow,

Squeezing with all my might,

Listening to the beat.

I am reminded that no matter what situations or challenges I face,

There is always hope.

This Hope can be described as a feeling of expectation

And a desire for a particular thing to happen.

Yes, my expectations are many,

I do anticipate a future with you.

My desire is that one day I will be yours, and you will be mine.


And as the raindrops get bigger and the sound of the rain on the roof

gets louder,

I am reminded of the thousands of butterflies that fill my heart each
day
As I anticipate hearing your voice on the other end of the line every
time I call
And when I hear your voice, though we are thousands of miles away,
It feels as if I am right in your arms

But it's not always like that, as sometimes the phones go unanswered.
Immediately thousands of questions race through my mind
Is he okay, or is he just having a bad day?
Is the workload just too much today?
I wish I was near to make it somewhat easier,
I hope by now he knows.

In my heart, all I do is pray, "Dear Lord, please keep him safe all
day."
Give him the strength and courage that he needs,
Remind him that you saved him just for me
And so as the rain continues to pour,
I will continue to bask in Hope
While trusting you to protect what we have,
I continue to enjoy this newness of life,
I will forever enjoy the rain.

# PROMISE

If I give you my heart, will you keep it safe?

And protect me from the pain of heartbreak?

If I give you my heart, will you promise to love me and not

compromise?

And promise me to be there for me through thick and thin?

If I give you my heart, promise me to always let the love of Christ

guide our very lives,

Will you promise to keep it forever?


I give you my heart; I will take yours,

We each have a responsibility to protect each other's hearts.

Together and with God's help, our hearts will become one

As we fulfill the master's plan.

I am not able to hide what I really feel inside,

As my heart is filled with butterflies,

I am thankful that faith and fate has brought us together

after twenty-four years.

# LOVE HOPES

---

You came into my life when I least expected

I was okay, well that's what I told myself

Down in my heart, I told God I needed a man

Not just any man, but one that would find me and love me first,

One that would not be afraid to express his love

A man I would love with all of me

One who will always seek after God's heart

One who values friendship and knows how to cherish this special gift
called Love

He would one day be my forever love

Trust me. I had stopped searching

I began to believe my preferred type no longer existed

I might as well set my mind free and learn to be content with only me

But then, you found me!


So thankful for modern-day technology,

Facebook messenger, to be exact,

Your friend request I accepted,

---

Though uncertain who it was.

Read your biography and realize we grew up in the same community,

After viewing your many photos, I remembered who you were

Back then, we never spoke; you watched me from a distance,

Too reserved to express how you felt, so you kept it all to yourself.

You thought you didn't deserve me; you didn't deserve my love.


What a joy it must have been when you finally realized,

This is your chance, win or lose; I must tell her how I really feel

You expressed how your heart felt it was exploding through your chest,

When finally, I accepted your friend request

Really, what could have caused this? I pondered in my heart

You said I should give you a chance, let's talk, and you will understand

For twenty-four years, you have been waiting,

To tell me how much you have always loved me.

Shocked at his response, I asked if he really meant me.

Why am I hearing all this just now?

With tears in his eyes, he said, "you will be my wife."

I will never ever let you go, not this time


Mesmerized by the statements you expressed,

I was left somewhat in awe,

I quickly erected my walls as I remember a few things from my past

How can you say I will be your wife?

When you know nothing of my present or my past?

Confidently you expressed your every thought,

I pinched myself to see if I was dreaming,

Is this all for real,

My God, I prayerfully seek


You expressed all you wanted in a wife,

And you knew it is in me, my goodness! Is this man for real?

Phone calls and text messaging now our daily routine,

Boy, you are not a bit shy to express your feelings,

your dreams, and your plans,

Long conversations have become a daily occurrence

You knew so much about me; I just couldn't understand

God, is he the one I have been praying for?

Lord Jesus, all the emotions that were dormant are now alive!

And I find it so hard to go one day without hearing your voice,

Your laughter and humor just brighten my days

I want to hear and see you as soon as I am awake

And at the end of every day

I enjoy praying with you and for you,

You are indeed a man after God's own heart.

You said, "take your time; I know it's so much to process,

Give me a chance and, you will soon understand."

I will protect your heart.

I will be there as we walk,

You will never be alone

It took some time for me to let you in,

But as I did, I knew you were the one,

Lord Jesus, I ask you to protect and cover us.

Lord, we give ourselves totally to you,

Order our steps and our love,

Lord Jesus, reveal to us everything that you have for us in your book,

Help us to be honest, true, and faithful.

Thank you for saving this fine gentleman for me and me for him.

Thank you for a second chance at life and love.

With grateful hearts, we say thank you, Lord.

# PULL BACK

Lord, you said, "Pull Back."

Yes, Lord, I heard you loud and clear, Lord what do you mean?

Those two simple words now resonate in my thoughts,

I pondered for an entire day

So many questions, thoughts all raced through my mind,

I need to understand fully what you ask of me

And so my thoughts led me to research those two magnificent words

"Pull Back"


When someone pulls back from an action, they decide to discontinue,

because it could have bad consequences

Your command is so strong,

Your words are loud and clear; pull back!

Let men run in pursuit after you; you are loved and lovable,

Sometimes one has to pull back, so they can be missed,

Listen, and you will learn,

Look, and you will see

Discern what is of me and what is not,

So you can understand the true meaning of this love


Stand back, watch, and you will see,

Pull back my child, let me do it,

It will be well done

Hard as it is, I will pull back,

I must allow you to do it,

You understand my every thought, and I know you want the very best
for my heart

Today, I fully surrender; I let you work while I pull back

# DISAPPOINTMENTS

Life is oftentimes marred with many disappointments that cause sadness, displeasure, and frustration of non-fulfillment of one's hopes or expectations, resulting in unhappiness. It is an uncomfortable space between our expectations and reality.

# PULLING BACK

For months these two words became my anthem,

I chew upon them in my thoughts,

I vocalize both words when I converse with my friends,

Two simple words with such profound meaning,

Applicable to all areas of one's life


My thoughts slowly transition into actions,

Pull back, step back,

Speak less, listen more

Words not often spoken but heard,

Be still in His presence and allow Him to speak

When we sit in quietness, we hear from God's heart,

On this journey, I need to hear His voice.

Lord, you have the map that will take me to my destination.


As the days turn into weeks and weeks into months,

These two words PULL BACK still resonate in my mind.

Each day I understand how powerful and deep they have become,

I am learning each day to let go and let God,

I am learning He is in control, and He sees ahead

Things do happen, and we do get anxious,

We are humans; we do err,

And so, at times, we must pull back

In order to lessen or stop the blows,

It is evident, the days ahead are unpredictable,

And because you spoke to my heart and I listened,

Nothing came as a surprise.

So when life gets complicated and uncertain,

Do remember these two profound words PULL BACK, you will never go wrong

My motto that will chart the way for my future endeavors

# START WELL!  END WELL!

Starting sometimes takes forever,

But when you do get the courage to start,

It brings a great sense of joy and happiness,

Depending on what lies ahead or the expected outcome

Here I was minding my own business,

When I heard these words clearly,

Start well, end well


What have I started or what will I be starting,

What will I be ending?

Thousands of questions raced through my mind,

Bombarded by my conflicting thoughts,

Often reminded by the parables Jesus spoke,

The truth is, I would love an explanation right away.


Starting all over can be very hard, especially when you worked from foundation up.

My gifts and ability were not mine to use as I please,

I clearly understood my life is a book,

To which many people will someday read,

I know that there are some who will not be able to read,

But will intensely look on as they are guided by me.

# DREAMS DEFERRED

Dreams deferred doesn't mean dreams denied,

These words echoed loudly in my ears,

I have come to realize that it doesn't matter what I did,

How dirty I am or how dirty you may think I am,

Or what mistakes I have made

I am still chosen.


It doesn't matter if people know or if they wrote me off,

It doesn't matter if I failed or if I didn't get it right,

It doesn't matter if I am first or even last,

It doesn't matter what labels you put on me,

I am still chosen.


My past is my past,

It's the life I leave behind,

My future is bright; I have nothing to hide,

You see, I was chosen before I was born.

God has the blueprint for my life,

He knows everything, no secrets, and no facades,

He loves me just the same,

Because He has CHOSEN me.

He chose me when no one else did or no one else could,

He carefully orchestrated my life from my conception,

He knew when I wanted to end my life,

The pain I felt was more than I could bear,

Yet, in a loving way, He held my hands.


He knows regardless; I must fulfill His plan,

He constantly reminds me by asking me the question,

Do you know you are chosen?

With reassurance and His unconditional love,

He reminds us that , He gave His life just for me,

He said the dreams I gave to you was my way of reminding you,

That though your dreams may be deferred,

They will never be denied,

Because I the Lord has chosen you.

# TOTALLY FREE

I am Totally Free!!

I chose to be Free!!

FREE to lift my hands...FREE to say amen...

FREE to know that today I can smile again

FREE

I am TOTALLY FREE because whom the Son sets free is free indeed

My marital relationships once kept me bound

Today, I use my voice to tell my story

I must break the silence on Christian infidelity.

I am free to openly share my moments of joy

And the events of sorrow experienced in my marriage while holding on to my faith in God.

At times I felt like a butterfly weaving its web

I wanted to be free from the cocoon of abuse, mistrust, hurt and un-forgiveness

Today I confidently say to those who believe

Regardless of what situation you are faced with

God is able to take them through it.

I can share my story because God has set me FREE

I am TOTALLY FREE because whom the Son sets free is free indeed

You too can also experience this FREEDOM.

# LIFE'S JOURNEY

On this journey called life,

Waiting is never our best friend or, better yet, best memory

The period of waiting can be viewed negatively,

Depending on who is in the picture, who the viewer is

Or what the viewer sees at that moment.

Humanly, as we all are, when life appears to be at a standstill,

We often feel useless, defeated, and deflated.

This process sometimes takes forever,

Hard as I try, it would appear I am not getting it right,

Could it be that my impatient self got the better of me?


Lord, I am interested in the destination,

I want to get to the end quickly,

The wait is too long,

Why can't I just walk under these hurdles?

And get to the finish line

Why do I have to jump?

That's harder and takes forever,

Can't you see, walking under is so much easier?

Each time I jump, a few hurdles are knocked down,

My feet get injured in the process, and my body aches,

This pain has now become excruciating


I am tired, I am frustrated,

It appears I will never be able to get to the end,

These hurdles are so challenging,

Each time I try, I constantly feel defeated

I feel stretched, the pain is now unbearable,

I am tired of trying,

Every fiber in me is telling me to give up


Lord, I know this is my test, and I must do my best,

You are interested in me and my journey,

Each hurdle is unique,

I know you are working on me,

But please

Help me to just get over this very last one

Each hurdle represents a test and the challenges associated with my life,

Each time a hurdle fell, I was delayed a bit.

Lord, you gave me the strength to actually pick it up and continue my race ahead,

I am reminded that the race is not for the swift but for those who endured to the end.

Help me to endure to the very end.

I might not be finished today,

The process to complete the journey is extensive,

There is so much I have learned.

Honestly, this race is not about speed but precision,

If I reached the finished line first or last,

I MUST meticulously plan my steps ahead,

In order to accurately execute your plans,

In a bid to complete my race.


I am learning to be patient with myself,

Though I fall, you quickly take me up,

Most importantly, on this journey of life, I can live in faith,

Knowing that at the right time,

God will get me to where I am supposed to be

You see, faith doesn't mean I know where I'm going on this journey,

It means I am trusting God, wherever He's taking me.

# I AM GRATEFUL

I am grateful that God hears me, and He is so good to me

In fact, let me tell you how good He is

He hears me before I call,

He knows what I need before I utter a word,

He hears my silence, my secret frustrations,

If I told people what I felt, it would scare them


They would judge me

Many would rebuke me,

But God isn't intimidated by what makes me insecure,

He hears me

And when I call Him, He responds

When I don't have words, God understands the things I don't say

God knows the needs that I don't mention


Isaiah 65: 24 states that before I call, God will answer, and while I am
yet speaking, He will hear

God anticipates my call, and His love is the basis

For granting my needs even before I ask

I am now able to see myself through the lens of His love for me,

I am grateful that God always hears me, and He is always so good to me.

# INTENTIONAL GOD

Intentional God,

Working out his intent will and purpose in my life,

What a week it was!

There are times when a day feels like a week and a month feels like a
year,

The month of August felt like years

So much has transpired in such a short time,

I believe our minds just cannot comprehend what exactly is
happening,

Two people who have not spoken in years

Now realize they cannot go a day without speaking to each other.


One thing we are sure of is that,

God allowed us to connect

So we can rediscover each other

I cannot help but think about you as I am awake,

And throughout my entire day

What a delight to hear your voice and to read your texts

Sometimes I feel as though my heart is bursting through my chest

Feelings that had died or I honestly didn't even know I had,

Are all racing to the foreground to be recognized

Hello there! In a bid to say we are all alive,

These feelings I certainly cannot hide,

Today I took the time to read over all your texts, to listen to every voice note you have sent,

Honestly, I have found more than a friend

Tears of joy ran down my cheeks,

I asked the Lord how long this wait will be?

How long can we truly stay apart?

And He quickly answered, not very long


While we both try to control our sexual feelings and urges,

Lord, we know we are weak, but you are strong,

As the days now turn into a month, we ask you, Lord, to continue to guide our hearts and our thoughts,

And to keep us safe from all harm.

Continue to knit our hearts together until we become one,

For you have kept him for me and me for him

Thank you Lord, for a second chance to love

And to demonstrate this love,

I believe we have found our soul mate

Together we watch as God work out His intent plans in your life

# MIXED EMOTIONS

What a roller coaster ride it was for us this week,

All our emotions were tested,

The questions were inevitable

With very few answers

The only comfort we have is found in God's word,

Being far away from each other in times like these is extremely hard,

My prayer is, Lord, please keep him safe from all harm,

Surround him with your presence,

And remind him you are with him.


Lord, my heart aches as tears flow uncontrollably down my cheeks,

All I wanted at this point was a phone call or text to confirm he is okay,

At least, I would know just how he felt and what was happening

I know it is very hard for him I must confess

But I felt angry as I expected him to call

I decided to put my fears and worries aside and focus on doing what I know I do best

And so I called on my prayer partners, and together we began to pray

Confident that everything is in God's hand.

What a relief it was to wake up to his text explaining why he didn't call

That explanation confirmed how much he really loves me

He didn't know how to explain all that was happening

And guess what babes, that's is okay


The Lord knows how much I adore this man

and believe me we are so much in love,

Nothing mattered to me at that moment,

I was just thankful he was ok, and I knew he would be just fine

Because his life is in God's hands.

The wait for results has been extremely hard, but faith tells us God is in charge.

I promise to hold your hand, and so, no matter what the results are,

I will be there with you, and that's just the truth.

Please don't shut me out; faith and love have brought us together,

we will get through this together.

I love you, and I can't wait to see you,

To hug, kiss, and squeeze you.

So keep the faith and continue to be you,

As we move forward with our relationship,

Confidently knowing one day,

we will be together as husband and wife.

# REFLECTION

Today was a day of reflection for me

I listened to music while I did my chores

As I listened, happy tears rolled down my face

I envision our lives together and anxiously wait for this to become a reality

Living in two different countries can be challenging but, I am grateful for technology.

It is our reality, and we both have to make it work at this time,

With God's help, all things are possible

Others have done it, and so can we,

You getting sick over the weekend really scared me

Tears rolled down my face; my eyes were swollen,

All I wanted to do was stay in bed

I prayed, I cried, asking God please just let him be okay,

Anxiety and nervousness kicked in,

My prayer was, oh Lord please be with him,

I knew something was wrong

As I missed my early morning texts and my phone call

I knew you were all alone in that truck,

I stayed up all night because I just could not fall asleep

What a relief it was when you called

You didn't say much, but I heard the pain in your voice,

I was really scared

I wished with all my heart that I was right there by your side,

I am so thankful that though we are thousands of miles apart,

God is right there with us no matter what

When we pray, He hears, and He answers

Our faith will be tested; we must entrust our lives into His hands,

Knowing He has brought us together and He is able to keep us together

Each day I am more and more convinced, God saved you just for me

Forgive me if I made you feel worse with my continuous texts and calls,

That's the only way I can show you my support when you are so far away

I hope that you felt my love and support and that you know all I do,

I do because you are no ordinary guy; you are my man

I love you with all my heart,

Take it easy, don't be too hard on yourself, use this time to rest and reflect

Our best days are ahead of us, and I do look forward to experiencing it all with you

I love you, and I can't wait for the day to come when we both say" I do" as we walk in God's plan.

# EMOTIONAL ROLLER COASTER

Happy, Sad,

Loved, Unloved,

Confident, Confused,

Open, Reserved,

Joyful, Anxious,

Thankful, Euphoric, Elated,

So many moments of emotion,

Some I can't even describe,

But honestly, I know what I am feeling inside

Loving someone is not always easy,

Especially when you want them to love you back too,

This can be easily misconstrued

Thousands of emotions surfaced daily,

Many questions yet, very few answers,

Moments of uncertainty

Filled with many fears

Days of highs and weeks of lows,

Tears of joy and pain,

Mixed emotions

Racing through my heart,

It feels like it is going to explode

This thing called love is so unpredictable,

One minute I want it, and the next moment I don't

Doubts and fears seem to be playing a game,

Should I let go and give it a try,

Should I open my heart one more time?

How will I know if he is the one if I pretend not to care?

Whose voice do I listen to?

Faith and trust must be applied,

God, you have given him to me

We both have agreed,

God, you have saved us just in time for each other,

The human side of us clearly seek an answer

Thousands of questions filled my mind,

Lord, I can clearly hear you say,

Take him or leave him,

Isn't he what you prayed for?

# HOPE

*It is that feeling of expectation and desire for a particular thing to happen. It is that feeling of trust and a desire for things to change and to also want that change so much. It is like making a wish and knowing it is going to come through no matter what.*

# I CAN ONLY IMAGINE

My days are filled with so many questions,

Lord, please help me to make the right decision

My heart is vulnerable,

I refuse to be hurt again,

Here I was taking care of my own life,

Having decided I might just stay single

I was tired of searching, didn't want to commit to anyone

That wasn't worth my time

Tired of these dating sites, Lord, I was actually done,

As I refuse to be hurt again


My focus was placed on my new love writing,

My job, my children, and just enjoying life.

I was fine, well, I guess as fine as I thought I could be

Out of nowhere came this handsome chap,

Who confesses that he has been waiting on me

I could only imagine

What my life would be with him

For months I felt as if it was a dream,

As all my prayers concerning a husband

Have now been manifested right before me

Ask, and it shall be given,

These things I have only told to you,

Right now, I can only imagine,

What my life will be if this is all you, Lord

I can only imagine finding a man that loves me like Christ loves the church,

I can only imagine me loving this man like I have loved no one else before

I can only imagine You bringing our families together,

We will live our lives to glorify You all our days

Love is of You and from You,

And when you are in it, it can only be amazing,

I can only imagine


Time will tell as I am often told,

Questions, fears, anxiety,

All rush through my mind

My friends say why not?

What do you have to lose?

Give him a try, as time will certainly tell

Lord, I can only imagine if this is your will.

# GOD'S WAY OR MAN'S WAY

Which way are you going to take?

Many years ago, I decided to choose GOD'S WAY

Was it an easy decision?  No.

Was it the right choice? Absolutely!!!

How has it been?

Certainly not easy, very bumpy at times,

I got lost so many times.

The path was not paved, some areas were very rocky and sometimes slippery,

I fell many times; I was bruised and wounded,

At times I walked off the path

Oh, there are so many times I got frustrated and decided I am going to choose "MY WAY."

But each time I came off the path and started "MY WAY," it got harder and more complicated, and I felt alone

I also realized that while I traveled "GOD'S WAY,"

I was never alone,

His word provided me with comfort and assurance that I needed

I realize that help is provided for me at specific points on the journey

When I got to the roadblocks, He always made a way

I honestly don't know how He did it, but the truth is, He did

I believe I am more than halfway on my journey

And though they are days when it is extremely hard and sometimes painful,

I know I made the right choice

I am confident that He who has begun a good work in me,

is able to complete it

I have no regrets about choosing "GOD'S WAY,"

clearly, we all have to choose,

Which way will you choose "YOUR WAY" or "GOD'S WAY"?

TODAY,  Make the right choice!!!

# BLOOM WHERE YOU ARE PLANTED

Bloom where you are planted!!!

Many thought I was dead because my root was attacked.

Oh, how they chopped my root, they even set it ablaze,

Little did they know that I was not dead.

There was still life left in me,

And though for years I appeared lifeless, I did not die.

You see, you cannot kill purpose,

Even when my root was destroyed,

Over time God stepped in, and life returned to my root.

I started to sprout in various places,

Before you knew it, I started to grow.

Trunk, stems, branches, and leaves appeared.

With the right soil, water and sunlight, I overcame the odds.

Though little in stature, I blossomed and bore fruits.

One's growth and success are not determined by man but by God.

"All wen dem chap di root out a di ground, yu nuh dead yet" don't you ever give up or give in.

I survived the odds and became a tall, strong tree.

I am becoming what the Lord has created me to be, a very strong tree.

# LIFE'S COCOON

The coffin of the caterpillar is also the birth canal of the butterfly,

I reflected on this for a moment and realized

How does this apply to my life?

You see, the caterpillar itself does not know it is going to become a butterfly,

It can't see what is happening to other butterflies.

The caterpillar thinks that it is dying

and begin to make its own coffin,

Then bam! Big surprise!!

It emerges from the cocoon,

With flashy new threads and some vibrant colours,

Amazing! Absolutely beautiful.

Well, maybe it is actually the same for us today,

We have no idea how beautiful we can be,

Unless we burst forth from our cocoon.

People then see how beautiful we are and marvel at our colours.

And so I conclude today, regardless of the odds,

I am determined to burst forth from my cocoon

And walk into my purpose

It's never over until God says it is,

It's all about your perspective.

# MISTAKES SHAPE OUR FUTURE

It's easy to look back and wonder, should I have done it differently?

I learn from my mistakes and apply them to future decisions.

I have learned not to judge yesterday's decisions with today's wisdom,

That will only paralyze me.

That momentum of shame will carry me to an even deeper place of despair.

God doesn't want me to do that,

He chose me, knowing that I would mess up.

Do I believe that?

Yes, I DO.

That's just the truth.

God said it, I believe it, and that settles it.

# TRANSFORMATION

Not for a minute was I forsaken; the Lord is always with me
The Lord is in my life
He never leaves me
So here I am, Lord
I am just not enough if you don't come
Come and show yourself mighty in my life
Those words played over and over in my heart
Meet me right where I am, Lord

You are all I want
Not for a minute, Lord, was I ever forsaken
You stood with me every step of the way
I lost my way; you found me
You redirected me
My steps you reordered
My thoughts you rearranged
My life you transformed

When I was empty, you filled me
Your light penetrated the darkness that was right before me
Your light paved my dark path
Lord your way, I now clearly see
You place your Holy Spirit in me
You turn my mourning into dancing
You turn my sorrows into Joys
You turn my sorrowful tears into happy tears
You have given me a new song
And a new purpose

I am totally free to become all you want me to be
I am not confused
I now know who I am
Sin no longer has dominion over me

I am free to become all that you have created me to be
Your truth is in my inward part
I will speak your word and declare your truth forever
Your word I cannot deny
I will passionately walk in obedience to your Word

# SECOND CHANCES

Not many people are privileged to experience second chances
Life is very unpredictable
The choices we make each day have consequences
Though sometimes oblivious to us
When done are oftentimes hard to handle
Had we known, we would have made better choices
God in His love and His mercies,
Does give His children second chances
This is a privilege we should not take for granted
Learn from your mistakes
Use them as stepping stones
Though we might not have the means at hand
To change our circumstances
We must be thankful
And welcome the second chances
A chance to prove that we will try
With all our strength and might
To change our ways, in an effort to make our wrongs right
And pull our weight again, in the race of life
Mistakes we will make and regrets we will have
But what determines a person's character aren't the mistakes we make.
But how we can take those mistakes
Turn them into lessons and not just mere excuses.
Let's accept the mistakes that we have made
Learn from them, set the stage
Let your inner strength burst forth with that
the fragrance of His amazing grace.

# BEING THE BEST VERSION OF MYSELF

I choose not to live a lie, trying to be someone else

I choose to do it right

By following God wholeheartedly and serving him diligently

I don't want to wake up one day with regrets for cutting corners

and living half-heartedly

I am mature and all grown up now

I have chosen to rise above men's expectations of me

And I will become the very best version of myself.

# TICK TOCK, TICK TOCK

Tick tock, tick tock,

Says the big clock

Quickly ticking away

Why do I have to do it now?

Why can't I wait?

I have all the time in the world, seasons come, and seasons go,

They change, and so does time, they often say.

Time and season are synonymous,

How will I know when it's the right time or the right season?

These questions I asked myself as I seek the answers.

The word of God clearly states in Ecclesiastes 3 verse 1-8

To everything, there is a season and a time to every purpose under the sun.

A time to plant and a time to reap

A time to kill and a time to heal

A time to laugh and a time to mourn

A time to love and a time to hate

A time to keep silent and a time to speak

A time to get and a time to lose.

There is definitely a place and time for everything,

And so it is with every season.

# TIME NEVER WAITS

Do today what you can,

Never put off today's task for tomorrow

As no one knows what tomorrow will bring,

Make hay while the sun shines.

Words echoed by almost every adult in my life,

Reminders that paved the way for my very life

As I grew to understand what these words really meant

Do it today and don't you wait,

As tomorrow rain might appear

And all our plans would surely be in vain.

Live in each moment and cherish each day,

Frolic in the sun and in the rain,

Enjoy the fragrance of each season,

Basked in God's amazing goodness.

Whether it is by seconds, minutes, or hours,

There is joy in knowing,

That you have completed what you actually planned.

# INTROSPECTION

*To exam or observe one's own mental and emotional processes while examining one's own conscious thoughts and feelings. As we analyze ourselves and our behavior, our goal is to gain emotional awareness so we can better understand how we impact others, be it negatively or positively.*

# LIFE STARES

I sat in the park

And just couldn't find myself doing anything else but stare

I watched as people parked their cars and disembarked

I noticed the look on their faces,

An air of melancholy surrounded some while others looked quite
happy

Some looked excited, and some just appeared to be nonchalant,

while others enjoyed the moment

As I looked on, my mind raced back to the days when we would take
our family to the park.

Yes, I said we, my husband and I.

The memories seemed like just yesterday,

I smiled, how happy and in love we were,

Creating memories that we wanted to last for a lifetime

Oh, how we had so many dreams and aspirations,

Not only for ourselves but also for our children

Some have materialized while others will remain dormant forever,

Time goes by so quickly

As I stared, there are moments when I smiled

As I reminisced on being young and in love

We were the couple who held hands

We hugged, we chatted, we laughed,


Regardless of what life throws at you,

Love and just live in the moment.

Appreciate and enjoy even the minute things in life,

Enjoy life, single or married,

With children or without,

Money or not

There is beauty all around

Take a moment, just sit and observe,

Bask in the silence, listen through the noise

Enjoy every moment, that's why we were created,

To inhabit earth while enjoying every single moment,

While life stares.

# I AM TOTALLY FREE

This morning while driving to work,

I asked myself the question, "what does it mean to be "Totally Free."

I don't believe there is one set answer for this question.

I believe that "Totally Free "will look different for each person.

But even though it looks different for everyone,

still, we all can achieve

I believe that our experiences in life and our beliefs

Are two reasons why we need to be free

Sometimes these beliefs are far from the truth,

Yet we attach ourselves to them,

And they become strongholds in our lives


At times we feel that we are not good enough,

We don't feel we are good looking enough

Or maybe, we don't feel we are worthy enough,

For years I felt that way.

My marriage did not help me to feel any better.

So today I can tell you that to be "Totally Free."

To me, it means just being able to wake up every morning

And loving the body that I am in

No shame, no guilt

And certainly not feeling like I need to look a certain way for anyone else

No more telling myself that I am not good enough

My appearance does not define my worth,

But my beliefs and actions do


"Totally Free" means,

I can now travel the world,

Experience a life full of nothing but new places,

New adventures

Meeting new people, forming new friendships,

I am now able to create lifelong memories

I am now able to walk in the freedom that God has given to me,

I am not ashamed of my past

I am able to forgive others, and I have forgiven myself,

I know that if I did not give my life completely to Christ, today I would not be "Totally Free."

I proudly wear my brand with confidence and, that's my testimony right there

I am TOTALLY FREE.

# THE CROSS

When I see the cross

I see His love

God, you love me so much that you gave everything, your only Son,

You did it all for me

I now have the opportunity to come boldly into your throne room,

To receive more of your grace and mercy,

Much more than I deserve

Jesus paid the ultimate price, one I did not deserve,

But His unconditional love makes all the difference

Lord, you did it unconditionally,

Demonstrating your infinite love,

No one in the entire world would have done what you did,

And so Lord, I receive your love

I honor you, Lord

I love and promise to keep your commandments

The cross today reminds me that regardless of my wrongs

You had the ultimate plan

All I need to do is to always repent and confess my wrong

Your forgiveness and restoration was all in the plan

Your death and resurrection testify of your undying love

And the plan you have for each of us

Yes!!! The cross reminds me of your priceless,

everlasting, never changing, never failing, unconditional love

# LORD CHANGE ME

Lord, your word is like a mirror,

My reflection, I clearly see

Remove the filters,

This is the real deal,

With all my heart, it is you I want to please,

Lord, you have all the power to bring about this change,

Here I am, please change me.

# GOD IS MY GUIDE

God desires us to walk in obedience to His word

His word is my compass, road map, guide, blueprint, and manual

There are so many times in my life when I was thrust into deep waters

Or I had a situation that I had no clue how I was going to get out of it

Or how I was to handle it

All I had was the word of God and

A little faith just to trust Him to work it all out.

I have learned that whenever I am not sure how things are going to work out

I should remind myself that I serve a God who always makes a way

A God who has my best interest at heart

He is working all things out in my life for His BEST and GREATEST good

His hand will forever be on my life as long as I stay under His covering

Thank you, Jesus. I couldn't have made it this far without you.

# HOLY SPIRIT, MY HELPER

Reading without glasses has become a challenge for me since I hit the forty marker

You can just imagine when my pair of glasses broke two weeks ago

Thankfully I was able to secure another pair

My glasses have now become my helper,

Yes, I need it to see, especially when reading.

I need to be able to read in order to carry out my task effectively and efficiently daily

Have you ever gone to the store, and you have to ask someone to read a label?

Yikes, certainly not a good feeling

That was me; I don't have my glasses. Can you please read this label for me?

Thankfully, the person chuckled and said, my mom is like that too

What a relief!!!

Two weeks of having no glasses, I was reminded that as difficult as it was for me without my glasses

It is even more difficult for me to live without the help of the Holy Spirit in my life.

The Holy Spirit is my constant helper

I need His help in every area of my life

Thankfully, God knew that before I was created, and so he gave me a personal navigator

A Helper who will never leave me stranded and confused

It was a challenge having to strain my eyes to read any print

But guess what?

Life is not always going to be a smooth ride

Come what may,

I will always have the Holy Spirit, who is my helper, working on my behalf.

# LEARNING TO FORGIVE

My Totally Free Journey has taught me many valuable lessons.

One that is most significant to me is FORGIVENESS.

I now understand that forgiveness doesn't mean pretending it didn't happen

But getting to that place where I make a deliberate decision

To let go of any feeling of resentment

I had towards the person or persons who have caused me hurt


It is never about if the person deserves my forgiveness

Neither does it mean forgetting

Forgiveness is deciding that I am not going to let un-forgiveness hold on to me anymore

It is also getting to that place where I forgive myself

So many times, we forgive others but not ourselves

I now experience peace of mind,

Freedom from anger, and I get to move on and enjoy life

# WHAT IS IMPORTANT TO YOU ?

So many things have been happening to me and to people around me

And so I am in a reflective mode

I have been waiting, listening, observing, and praying

I woke up this morning with this thought on my mind

"People make time for the things that are really important to them."

What does this mean?


Time is something I have been thinking about lately

There never seems to be enough of it at any time

It's ironic; time is one thing you can't just go out and get more of

It's one of the things we have to be very careful about giving away

We might all be very busy, but I do believe it all comes down to
priorities

If you are a priority to someone, they will make every effort to make
time for you

I do believe we can always make time for what is important to us


Knowing and understanding what is important makes the difference.

We all have the time

It's just how we choose to allocate our time

To the things that we care about the most in this world

Think about it, who or what do you make time for?

Is it your spouse, is it your husband or your wife, is it your children,

Is it your family, is it your job, or is it your car, is it Jesus?


Who or what is your priority today?

I believe when you love someone or something

They become your priority

Many things are not equal in life,

But everyone gets the same 24 hours a day, 7 days a week

We have the innate ability to make time for what we truly want

Let's do the right thing

Life is short - so don't waste it.

# WHO VALIDATES ME ?

For years I felt that all the good I ever did was never noticed

I felt no one saw me for who I really was

I felt I was the least valuable among all the jewelers' pieces

I was never placed at the front of the showcase

I was always at the back

I just never felt valuable

And so for years, I searched for man's acceptance of me

I wanted to be seen as one of the valuable pieces


Anger, frustration, disappointment

Were the least of how I would describe how I felt

For years all I did was my very best

I gave up so much, yet no one saw

I felt unappreciated even by my very own

I tried so hard to hide all this inside

But there were many times my anger came out as fury

I would lash back; my defense mechanism was up

They would just stand back and watch or just attack

You don't understand what I went through and what I gave up

I felt so deserted; all I wanted them to see was that I was just as valuable as the other pieces

My mind was filled with so many negatives

The enemy had me on his playing field

And all I could hear was his subtle remarks, you are not good enough

And so the rejection kicked in and said attack, attack, attack

For years I built my wall of defense; many tried to enter

But they just couldn't get in

What did I do wrong?

Why do I feel this way?

I did my very best, yet no one saw

It was hard, I must confess

But I truly did it all from my heart


My actions have become noticeable

And so no one wanted to be around me

My humble persona eroded

And anger was my portion for the day

I often lashed out for the simplest things

Many felt scared to communicate as the simplest word could set the whole conversation ablaze

Many pulled back as my attitude and actions changed

They felt my pain, and I felt the shame

Why am I the one to feel this way?

When all I did was done from my heart

All I wanted was to be validated

Just for one person to say, yes!!! You did it

Little did I know, I was already validated

By the one who created me from the very beginning

The one who was there every step of the way

The one who knows every intent of my heart

The one who forever carries the seal

And gives approval when he is pleased


How could I miss that?

Man's validation of me is temporal

They can only see what's on the outside

Their opinions are sometimes skewed, and some remarks are never
true

The clutter of life sometimes blinds their very eyes

And the results are far from the truth


After years of seeking man's validation

I later learned the truth,

one validation that matters comes from the one who created me

And who has the blueprint for my life

The one who refines me daily

And filters out the muck

The one who has designed me to be the finest piece in his collection

I am uniquely placed just right where I am supposed to be

The authenticity of his validation

Will stand the test of time

His stamp of approval seals the deal

I am much more precious and valuable than they will ever know

And only my maker will reveal my true value

I am indeed a rare but unique and precious piece

And today I declare, yes!!!

I am validated by the one whom I love, and he is none other than

GOD.

# SURPRISES

Today I am stronger than I thought

Today you are stronger than you thought

I was not quite ready for what God was doing

But guess what?

It is here!

Surprise!

He was ready for me


Bam, I had no clue what to expect

His word I obeyed

Sometimes I stumble, while sometimes I fall

Oftentimes saying, Lord, I am just not ready

But in that still small voice

I hear Him saying, I know you are not, but I am ready

Surprise!


All of my uncertainties

All of my shortcomings

All of my failures

All of my struggles

All of me I give to you,

I know I am safe in your hand

Lord, you are so full of surprises

I just cannot keep up with you

You promise you will never leave me

And you will work everything out for my good

Surprise!  You did it

Just as you promised


I am chosen, and I am loved by you

Eyes have not seen, and ears have not heard

What you, my God, has in store for me, your child

My past didn't kill me

It made me stronger

My life for all to see

Surprise!!!

Yes, Lord, you did it

To you, I give all the Glory.

# FREEDOM

*The power or right to act, speak or think as one wants. It is the choice to live your life doing what you want, to live where you want, to eat by choice, and to learn what your heart desires. It is about ensuring respect and not living free. It is a sequence of decisions we make every day, whether they are big or small.*

# WHAT SEASON ARE YOU IN ?

Winter, spring, summer, and autumn

Each with its own specific season

Uniquely designed by the master

To capture the beauty of His creation

Season changes, and so do our lives

One can't help but question why

What season am I really in?


As I reflected on this question

I realize I had a choice

I can work my best in each season

Enjoying all the bounties of this time

I can use my gifts to capture and create great memories

I never wish to hide

Or I can sit idle and remain stuck in one season while the others pass
me by

What season am I in?

Ready or not, the season's come without requesting my approval

It does what it was designed to do


Summertime it's playful outside

Warm temperature compels you to take a swim

Winter comes, and all we want to do is hide inside

Oftentimes not ready for the chills and discomfort it sometimes brings

Snuggle up and get cozy

For what tomorrow brings


How ironic, its autumn, and all the leaves just disappear

It would seem as if a hurricane just came

People and animal's scampers to find warmth

In unison, for once, we agree


Springing into spring

With all that we have

New expectations and anticipations

Trusting the creator to fulfill his plan

Seasons change, and people do too

Such a pity,

People don't change the same way as the seasons do

Seasons are predictable

People are unpredictable,

We easily change our minds

People will never be like seasons

I guess that is what makes us so unique

Seasons are filled with secrets

That reminds us of the power of the perfect work of Christ

What season are you in?

# PRUNING SEASON

Are you in your pruning season?

This is necessary for consistent growth

When there is pruning, one should expect some shedding

Some breaking and bending

Which can oftentimes cause pain

Allow the master to do his pruning

By removing all the lifeless prongs

That create hindrances in one's lives

After the pruning, new life begins

New yields that will result in a great harvest.

# FRAMED BY YOUR WORD

Lord continue to steer my life,

You are the captain of my ship,

I surrender completely to you,

I step back; you are my guide,

You lead, and I will follow

My world is framed by your words,

So Lord, please speak through me,

Remove every distraction,

It's only you I want to please.

I will keep my eyes and my heart on you,

Give me the boldness to speak,

Let my conversation be seasoned with salt,

If salt loses its taste, everything becomes tasteless

Lord help me to be slow to speak but quick to listen,

Guide my heart and my thoughts.

I am your tool ready to be used,

Take your place as all will see,

My world will forever be framed by your Word.

# ENDLESS LOVE

I have always believed that true love was somewhere out there

Waiting to be found.

This love exists and, when found, should be cherished,

Even if it's the rarest thing in this world,

I am happy that love found me


I was given a chance of love for a second time,

This means a lot

I had no idea I was able to love again until love found me

This feeling I just can't hide,

It feels like everything I often sit and daydream about,

It's everything all at once,

It's the love that you fall in

The love you work so hard not to fall out of

It's the love that makes it so easy to say I am sorry, I forgive


A love that's enormous and so strong,

One that never fades or loses its authenticity

This love is potent; it is tangible,

Our hearts are attracted to each other from the very start.

It wasn't physical attraction as we were miles apart,

Our hearts connected the moment we spoke,

Like magnets, we were drawn together.

Our words flowed effortlessly as we communicated

We laughed with and at each other.


These moments we will cherish forever,

It's the love we dream of,

One that's considered great,

It's the love you fight for regardless,

This love is definitely from God.

# UNDEFEATED CHAMPION

Even though He did no wrong

On a cross, He was hung

They thought they could silence Him

That would be His end

So they nailed Him to the cross and crucified Him

Little did they know

It was all in the resurrection plan


So humble He came to earth

With no intentions of His own

All He wanted was to fulfill His Father's plan

That would eventually bring Hope to man

And so He spent His days

Teaching His Father's Word


The ignorance of many He just couldn't understand

Nevertheless, with great love

He obeyed His father and fulfilled His plan

Hidden secrets He would reveal

Many were shocked at His humility

Words of wisdom flowed

Like fountains of refreshing water

Many valuable lessons He taught

By sharing stories, parables, and the life He lived

The analogies He used are still true today

They stand and prove that

Jesus is the undefeated champion


He gave us Hope

No one will ever be able to give

And yet many just could not understand

That He was God's only Son

The undefeated champion

The infallible one

Who died to redeem us all

You and I are bought with a price

It cost Him, His life,

He could not remain dead

The scriptures must be fulfilled

The champion of champions

From the grave, he arose triumphantly, undefeated.

Over two thousand years

We have come to one conclusion

His death was imminent

He could not be held captive forever

He had the power over death and hell

He overcame and conquered

He who was dead is now alive

He is the risen one

Who sits at the right hand of His Father

Continuously making intercession for each of us.


Open your hearts to Him

Let him unlock His truths in your heart

Oh, taste and see the salvation of the Lord

Trust His word; it is truth

His plan for us His children

Will lead us to His Father

A kingdom He is gone to prepare

So one day, we will be with Him

Jesus, the undefeated champion

Reigns forever and forever.

# JESUS PERSONIFIED

For God so loved the world

Yes, that includes you and I

He gave His son, His only Son

Who came to earth with just one plan

To redeem us all from Satan's clan

His love for us was motivated by compassion

For just about everyone

His strength and resilience stood the test of time

His character epitomized that of His Father

Faultless, perfect, exemplary meticulous, impeccable, and spot-on


Choose today who you will serve

This decision cannot be forced

The scriptures must be fulfilled

Though tempted and tested by Satan

Jesus stood His ground

Looked Satan in his face and truthfully declared

I am here to do my Father's will

Man shall not live by bread alone but by every word that proceeds
from the mouth of God

And as if that was not enough

Satan took Jesus high up on the mountain

Offered Him everything

To trade His worship to him


Hmmm

What disrespect to our King

You stood in honour to your Father

You did not yield; you stood your ground

Declaring the truth

By now, Satan would have concluded

All our worship belongs to our King


Little did he knew what belongs to your father

Also belongs to you

Another defeat Satan suffered

It's final, Jesus won

Worship belongs only to our King

Jesus our Lord personified


And so it had to come to this

You had to die the cruel death

Accusations came as you spoke the truth

Not everyone wanted you dead

Your disciples wanted you to be with them to the very end


I can just imagine how broken they were

When they realized the end was near

Despite the sadness

It was comforting to know

The Holy Spirit, our Helper, was left to carry on the show

You died that mankind could live

To be free from the chains of sin

Humble you came to earth

Took on the cloak of humanity

Demonstrating humility

Poised with love and grace

Gently and caring

Correcting in Love

Compassionate and meek

Filled with wisdom

All from above


Upon a tree, you were hung

Not because of what you had done

Demonstrating your undying love

A crown of thorns was press upon your head

Many jeered and mocked

They flogged you

Your body bore the scars

The wounds inflicted reminds mankind today

The sin base of our lives you clearly changed

Freedom from the terror of Satan and his schemes

Repent and confess our sins

Believe in our hearts

That Jesus died and rose again

We all have a chance

To be saved and to be with Him on His second return.

That is all he asked.

# MOVING FROM HURT TO HEALING

When we are going through a hard time

It can be very difficult to let other people in

Healing looks different for everybody

But it is a process that is better when we show up for each other

We all need each other

It's never easy to stand alone

When there is pain and hurt

Amidst the dismal look

There is hope on the horizon

Your pain is not unique to you

You must never give up

Know that your faith will carry you


Moving from a place of hurt to a place of healing

One must truly get to the place

Where they forgive those who have caused the hurt

As this is the foundation that breaks one free from their tormentors

It's very easy to be stuck in the cycle of frustration

It's never easy to forgive

The memories from the pain of hurt easily attached itself to us

While the process of forgiving

Sometimes rehash these memories


Forgiveness is not pretending it didn't happen

But getting to that place

Where one makes a deliberate decision

To let go of any feeling of resentment towards the person who has

caused the hurt

It is never about if the person deserves your forgiveness

Neither does it mean forgetting

It is also getting to that place where you also forgive yourself


You see, hurt has no colour, no age barrier

Hurt is no respecter of persons

Neither is hurt unique,

In this journey called life

Everyone goes through some form of hurt

Don't be despaired

Amongst your fears, doubt may arise

Protect your heart if you must

But always remember, despite your hurt

Our heavenly Father has already made a way.

# REWRITE YOUR STORY

Have you told yourself that the story of your life is never going to be any different?

Have you wondered if this is all it can ever be?

You constantly ask why me?

Guess what, you are not the only one

Your story isn't over.


God often brings unexpected blessings in unlikely places.

Keep looking the cardinals are there

Set your eyes like a flint

It might be hard to see it right now

One day the truth will be known


You are strong enough for today

God's plan for your life is more than you can imagine

Strength comes from within

Stop for a moment

Life experiences build strength

It is developed along the way

Keep going,

You have just enough for the next step

With Gods help and your determination

You can rewrite your story

# TIME WASTED

Time wasted can never be regained

If you sleep more, that doesn't make up for the sleep that was lost

Opportunities available today might not be tomorrow

Now don't get me wrong

I am a big fan of thinking things through before acting

but sometimes we think for too long

until there is no longer something to think about

And we miss the bigger plan


It is our nature as human beings to look back at our past with regret

We often iterate and make insinuations that we will never do this or that again

But truth be told, we do the same thing over and over again

Our human nature will always be with us

Mistakes will be made, and you will not always win

There is no defeat in your past that can lessen God's view of you in the future.

Sometimes we hold ourselves hostage to our past

We spend our days thinking,

How could I have done better?

Or why did it happen to me?

Why didn't I see that coming?

I am here to remind you that there is a reason for all of this

And that's why it is called your past

That chapter is closed

God wants you to see yourself through the lens of His love

For you and your future,

Not your past.

# FRESH START

Begin to put things in place

To give birth to your new season

Pay attention to what is in your present

It's a new day for new opportunities

It's a new day to fulfill your dreams

Choose a new pathway

Create new footprints

Begin to listen to the quietness among the noise

Anticipate and work towards your future.

Don't let your attachment from your past

Keep you from trusting God in the present

When one door closes and another opens

Bringing bounteous promises along

A new opportunity means a fresh start

Embrace and enjoy your fresh start

Enjoy and bask in all the wonderful benefits

Provided to you by the Father

New possibilities

New beginnings always yield new fruits.

# FORGIVENESS

*It is the action or process of forgiving or being forgiven. It is a conscious, deliberate decision to release feelings of resentment or vengeance toward a person who has harmed you, regardless of whether they deserve your forgiveness. It does not mean forgetting, nor does it mean condoning or excusing the offenses.*

# HOW DID I FIND MYSELF?

I found myself when I REPENTED AND SURRENDERED

my heart and my will to the Lord

I found myself when I understood that God did not see me

like how man sees me,

And that regardless of what I DID OR DIDN'T DO, He loves me

And His love is and will always be available to me.

I found myself when I STOPPED blaming everyone and

everything

I found myself when I forgave myself,

I decided that I am not going to let un-forgiveness hold onto me

anymore


I found myself when I decided I can no longer thrive in

Rejection, so I had to let it go

I found myself when I released those who hurt me,

I found myself when I decided I was going to live and not die

I found myself when I became honest with myself

I found myself when I started to trust God

I found myself when I understood that my destiny is

determined by my decisions

I found myself when I understood that I had options

My feet cannot take me where my mind has never been

I found myself when I realized I am not a victim of my circumstances

I found myself when I recognized that enough was enough

And did something about it

I found myself when I recognize and understand

That I am fearfully and wonderfully made

I found myself when I began to share my story and my testimony

# A WOMAN OF STRENGTH

Woman

Uniquely created

Blessed with the gift of giving

And such willingness to help others

She consoles others even though she herself is hurting

Fearless, forgiving, faithful

Strong, smart, skillful

Godly Woman

Resilient

Matriarch of our Society

Caring, competent, creative

Woman of worship, worth, wisdom

Woman of wealth

The stalwarts and backbone of our society

Epitome of greatness

Inspiring

Far from perfect, yet humble to acknowledge her wrong

Self-less

Loving enough to say "I forgive you."

Confident

She is at peace with herself

There is no need to prove herself to anyone

Woman

She values her self-worth and reminds other women of theirs

She is not ostentatious but instead

Presents herself just as she is

A woman of character

**A WOMAN OF STRENGTH!**

# THE FRAME IS AS IMPORTANT AS THE PICTURE

Today I got a chance to choose my frame

No one can make that decision for me.

I can choose to frame my picture with frustration or favor.

I can choose to define all the negatives or

Positives that really impacted my life

Both decisions are mine

And will determine the outcome of my life

The negative events sometimes lead to mountains of frustration

While on the other hand

Positive attitudes oftentimes lead to favor

With careful analysis

I can choose favor over frustration

My choice of frame is not determined by popularity

And by no means appearance

Experiences along with life-long lessons

Influences my decision

With so many different frames to choose from

I truly understand that I have the ability to choose

The perfect frame for my picture

The frame that will resonate with my audience

One that will express my ideas and thoughts within the frame

I also realize once I select the frame

I can begin to paint my picture

Ensuring everything I say is relevant and consistent within that frame.

As I do believe the frame is as important as the picture

Choose your frame today and start painting your picture.

# UNIQUELY CREATED

I had a very interesting conversation with my dad
It was about how different each of his children were
They are numerous adjectives that can be used to describe each
Vivacious, victorious, feisty, faithful, friendly
We oftentimes converse about the traits that we have
that can be easily identified in our parents
We usually erupt in crazy laughter

Gregarious, extrovert, impulsive, sympathetic, industrious
Loving, caring, sensitive, kind
Just to name a few of the outstanding traits that define each sibling
Each child holds a special place in our parent's heart
Seven brothers, seven different minds
A very popular but true adage
You see, I have two brothers and four sisters
Our personalities and roles are all so different

We are like the ingredients to my favourite sweet potato pudding
All the ingredients for the pudding
Are equally important
If these are not all added in the process

At the right measurement and proportion

The end result will be tasteless

The whole conclusion all the ingredients are vitally important

Each different in taste and texture

Blended together to create the most amazingly delicious pudding


When my siblings and I come together

It is always the beginning of something great

We have grown to understand that working together

Creates harmony and success

We may not have it all together, but together we have it all

Coming together creates an amazing bond that results

In cherished memories and sincere friendships

That none of us would trade in this lifetime

Kudos to my remarkable parents and siblings.

Unified together, creating the most amazing selfless family.

# NO MORE FAÇADE

Keeping it real

No more facade

What's the sense?

Trying to please everyone all my life

While inside, I was dying

It's about time I keep it real

This constant arguing and fighting

When will it end?


Pulling me here, there, and everywhere

Unhappy I am, yet no one sees

As I masked it all behind a smile

We mirrored the perfect couple

But that was far from the truth

We have grown so far apart

Not only in the distance

But in heart

Yes I am keeping it real

No more facades

At the end of the day

It's about how I feel


Keeping it real

For all to see

It's in our human nature

Wanting to please everyone

Truth be told, we can't

Not even Jesus could


Aim to be grounded

Know you worth

Use your voice

Everything you go through today

Will make room tomorrow

If we could only be true to ourselves

We would have ended this a long time ago

Lessoning the pain and hurt


It's a tough decision

One we never forecasted

Unpredictable

Heartbreaking

Years of time, money, and heart

Was totally invested

Always praying for a happy yield


Let's keep it real

So many years elapsed

Trying to fix it here, there, and everywhere

It always got back to right where we started

I can't do this anymore

Yes, I know what the Bible says

I know what the churches teach

And I know my pain

I hate to break the rules

I must save myself

I cannot continue to live a life of lies

It will eventually lead to my end

My demise


So yes, I am keeping it real

It's over, yes, that's my final decision

In order to live, I must let you go.

I might not have the power to control all that is happening to me

But I do have the power to leave.

# LOVE ME FOR ME

Love me

Love me for who I am

Not who you think I should be

Love me, for me

Why do you want me to be like someone else?

I am one of a kind

Beautifully and uniquely created by the most high.


Why do you want me to change to fit your childhood fantasies?

This is reality

I cannot look the same way I looked when we first met

C'mon back then I was not stressed

And neither did I have an entire household to be kept

My body went through two pregnancies

Not to mention two C-section surgeries

And after all of this,

You want me to still look the way I looked at twenty.

Love me, for me

Do not shame my body

I have been through so much

I would love to go to the gym

But instead I had to choose to pay the bills

I would love to change my diet

But that also comes with a cost

I really thought this was a partnership

Little did I know there was a price to pay!

After two pregnancies, can't you love me, for me?

Love me, for me.


Droopy and saggy tits

Are a result of the choice I made to breastfeed our kids

Remember you said the breast is the best

When I opted to switch, you made a big stink of it

Flaps here and there, love handles no longer hidden

Stretch marks that resemble the maze at the park

After all of this, you still expect me to look just the way I looked when

I was twenty


Love me for me

I cannot join your silly games

I have to love me for me

Life continues with or without you

I have a choice

Regardless of how you feel

My body continues to change

And I must love and appreciate me

I am proud of who I am

And who I have become.

I am proud of how I look

And when I see our children

I have no regrets

My body was the home for two amazing kids

And so I am happy with me

I am happy that my body is changing

That's the whole purpose of growth

So guess what, it's okay

My body is my reality.

I will continue to love me

And I am proud of my body

I will continue to love me for me.

# UNRESOLVED CONFLICTS

You took my silence for granted

I got so tired of fighting

I got so tired of arguing

I got so tired of all the nagging

The lies, the pretense

The unresolved conflicts


I got so tired of your games

You saying you were there when you knew you were not

Calling your phone and you could hardly speak

Fearing I would know exactly where you were

Your deceit caused me so much pain

Your consistent lying or half-truths, as you would often say

Contradicts with your very beliefs

Mixed with disrespect for me and our family

Enough is enough

And when I told you

You didn't believe me

And so I just stop speaking

Terrible anguish struck my heart,

I felt a dreadful ache as if something was being torn inside me

And I was slowly dying.

In my heart, I knew this was not for me

You took my silence for granted

Believing I would stay forever.

# DEAR MOM

Dearest Mom, as a little girl growing up, you were our role model

I said our because

You weren't mom to just my four other siblings and I,

But mom to our cousins, your younger siblings

And the many other children that you came in contact with daily

You were our big-time chef, our doctor, our mediator,

Our prayer warrior, our teacher, and our friend

You name it, my mother was that and more to all of us.

My mom was always there

Whenever we needed a shoulder to cry on,

Or needed just a simple reassurance of "yes we can."

She was our cheerleader who never gave up on anyone or any given task

I knew that regardless of her many screams and shouts

Her love for us was much bigger than her little heart

How did she manage to handle it all?

How did she manage to maintain a smile and not a frown?

How did she manage to Mek di likkle money stretch?

How did she do it?

Growing up as little girls

We would sometimes daydream

Oh, how we wanted to be like our mother

To have children of our own

And to maintain a well-kept home

As soon as we got a doll or whether it was the grass that we pretended was our doll

We would role-play our mom

Pretending we were the mom, and our dolls were our children

I remember vividly how we would dress up our dolls

Wanting them to look as beautiful as our mom made us look


As girls, our motherly instincts kicked in from an early age

As we grow, our mom's task seemed effortlessly

She would basically do the very same thing over and over every day

Not complaining for a minute

Doing each task with such pride and joy

My mother was the one that kept the house together

Hard as it was or tired as she was

She exuded her duties with grace and pride regardless of

In our eyes, motherhood looked easy

And so our dreams began from an early age

We all wanted to be like our mom

To have children of our own,

To raise families that would carry on our parent's legacy

My mom encouraged and taught us to be the best versions of ourselves.

And no one else.

She taught us to work hard and to be independent

This, she demonstrated all her life.


When I became a mom and had a family of my own

I quickly learned that this job was by no means an easy one

I realized it took lots of dedication and commitment

Denying both needs and wants

Sleepless nights, anxious moments

Mixed with joy and happiness

Many times motherhood leaves you with no choice

How did my mom do it?

I just can't comprehend

I only have two children

She had five plus the many more

There were so many times when I literally gave up in my mind

I felt I was going to crash under the weight

I now realize our mom's tasks were not as easy

As they appeared in our childlike eyes

Many sacrifices were made

Being a mother means being completely and totally overwhelmed at
times
In some of the best possible ways, one can imagine
Motherhood means sleepless nights, temper tantrums
Wiping running noses while kissing cuts and bruises
Markings and scratches on every piece of furniture
Finger-painting on the wall and tons of big belly full of laughter,
While constantly preparing healthy and nutritious meals,
right around the clock.
Motherhood has made life more colorful
Than I ever knew it could be.


Being a mother means I have two little people who walk around with
My heart and soul in the palms of their sweet, smudgy hands.

Being a mother means I get to see all the possibilities in the world
Through my children's eyes

I work so hard to be the kindest and most generous version of myself
to them

So that my children can look up to me each day

Just as I looked up to my mother.

Being a mother means being tired,

Sometimes grumpy and never left alone

It means being funny, loving, and caring

While enjoying every moment spent with my children

Realizing that eventually they will grow up

And it would be completely worth it.

Motherhood is a lifetime adventure

The hardest job you will ever do without getting a single cent

But one that I can unequivocally say

Is by far my greatest achievement to this very day

And so I proudly say to my mom, you did an amazing job

You epitomize the virtuous woman highlighted in Proverbs 31,

Her children rise up and call her blessed.

Her husband also and he praises her.

Many daughters have done virtuously, but thou excellest them all.

Hats off, take a bow; you definitely outdid yourself Mommy Dorothy.

**Dedicated to my mother Dorothy DaCosta**

# SOCIETAL ILLS

Crime, violence, and abuse are now out in everyone's full view

The public cries as this appears to be the new norm

Cold, callous and heartless are mildly terms used,

To describe the perpetrators

Crime, abuse, violence, buggery,

Rape, kidnapping, robbery, murder

The age group varies not

Perpetrators just attack

While the innocent sometimes become the victims

Who will address the societal ills?


Crime, violence, and abuse cut across all,

Political, social, economic

Ethical, psychological, and cultural divides

All these elements are inter-related

And affect the fickle framework of our society

The ethos of our country

Mirrors a culture of crime, violence, and abuse

Many faithfully embrace the adage "see and blind, hear and deaf."

Resulting in many of the societal ills we are now faced with

Very complex and detrimental

Leaving us with no immediate or overnight solution.


It's no longer a secret

Hidden behind closed doors

Or beneath the sheets

Women, men, and children feel powerless

And in order to win

Some suffer in silence while others resort

To their defense mechanism

Who will address these societal ills?


The sin base of our lives

Has dominated our very thoughts, emotions, and decisions

God gave us His original plan

From the beginning, God knew if we follow and obey His plan

Then our end would not be dread

Crime, abuse, and violence subsequently was not in his plan

When love becomes hate

And the pain gets great

Leaving no place for hate to recalibrate

The pain and anger turn into rage

Fueling a fury of emotions

That sets a forest ablaze


The price tag is high

As much was invested

No one wants to lose

Hearts have become hardened

From years of pain, hurt, and trauma

Someone should pay, and now the bloodletting continues

Crime, abuse, and violence have now become the reality of many

Political leaders now realize societal ills do affect everyone

They grope about trying to find the solutions or at least a workable

plan


Church leaders are called upon to pray and to seek Gods divine

intervention

Families are scared and some traumatized for years

Men and women

Boys and girls

Teenagers all suffer from these gruesome and deadly attacks

Homes filled with fear, while the pain becomes great

Paralyzing and killing the purpose

One was created for

While societal ills influence the future.


How can people live and thrive in a society

That is filled with constant abuse, crime, violence, and the killing of

our people

Shattering dreams and hope

While the perpetrators walk around with no remorse

No empathy

No respect for the laws of the land or the security forces

Respect for life has become obsolete

We are no longer our brother's keeper

This mayhem must come to an end

Enough is enough

Let that be our societal cry


Murder, abuse, and violence does affect everyone

Let's use our voices, public awareness outcry

We all have rights; no one should suffer

Speak up, speak out

Let our voices be heard right across the land

Let's call it what it is, wrong

Acceptable rights we defend

Let's not succumb to these scums.


We must take a stand as

The stench of crime, violence, and abuse fill the air

Our morgues tell the tale

While families feel the pain

And our leaders continue to struggle to address societal ills


Let's come together in a unified front

Violence and crime will no longer dictate

Enforce the laws and punish the perpetrators

Reward the law-abiding citizens in the land

Every action does have consequences for us and for others.

Do unto others as you would want them to do unto you

Abuse varies but is not unique

Help is available to all who seek

The abuser and the victim can both be free

Together we can break these deadly cycles of

Abuse, violence, and crime

And put an end to our societal ills and mayhem.

# EROS LOVE

Don't take the word love lightly

These four letters run very deep

It is much more than a feeling

That is here today and gone tomorrow

Eros love of which we speak

It is more than butterflies in your stomach

And those nerve rocking jitters

This love is addictive, and humans just can't get enough of it


This love is the catalyst that provokes one's feelings of attraction to the other

Like every other word

The word love is easy to enunciate

Yet many find it hard to communicate

It is not only what you say

But also what you do


This love is more than that feeling of intimacy

That lights your romantic fire

And sends your scurrying for cover

It is more than that kiss you wish you would never miss

This love is more than the ecstasy

That sometimes tickle your fancy

Leaving you with limited options


This love is Eros love

Passionately displayed through physical attraction

Admiration and romantic affection

This love creates room for you to know your partner

And vice versa


This love brings two individuals together

Committing to becoming one

Understanding that their lives are now a partnership

While patiently learning about each other

This love is understanding neither is it perfect?

Yet working cohesively to perfect each other

It's a beautiful love all should desire

And most definitely never take for granted.

# PANDEMIC WOES IN OUR EDUCATION SECTOR

Shocked, Scared

The world was not prepared for anything like this

A pandemic of this magnitude

Unexpected

Life defined by many was great or good

People were living; dreams were fulfilled

Freedom

There was an air of achievement and accomplishment

Regardless of the challenges or setbacks

Dreams were accomplished

We maneuvered them

Hope

Resilience, strength, determination

Are our hallmark.


Instantaneously with little or no warning

Bam, just like that

COVID 19 pandemic hit the entire world

Upended the lives of children and families, including Jamaicans

While crossing virtually every key measure of childhood development

Gravely affecting every family

Including our education system

Chaos, confusion, frustration

Are mild description of what our reality is

Inadequate resources

Government Leaders, Administrators, Principals

Teachers, parents, students

All seeking immediate answers

Finger points to one solution

Implementing virtually appropriate programs

For the nation's children in the fourteen parishes of Jamaica

Where internet access is inadequate, unstable, and unreliable.


Over the year, numerous challenges have arisen

Among the nation's most precious and vulnerable

Our children

Faced with hunger, isolation, anxiety, depression

Poverty, death, and abuse

All have increased significantly

As our children cry foul play

Access to learning environments, socialization, essential services

Health, nutrition, and protection has decreased

More and more, the impact of social isolation

Influences the loss of social skill development

Generating trauma on our children

Who desperately need devices and internet access

To navigate their online lessons

And to thrive in the digital landscape.


The scars our children bear

Will be inevitable from this pandemic for years to come

Addressing those scars is an urgent priority.

Providing access to high-quality education

Is not the singular solution to these problems

But a major cornerstone

The financial challenges expressed by many to secure a device

Limited or no internet connection

Accessing online platforms daily

Coupled with the inability of some parents to assist students with their online work

While they themselves focus on making ends meet

Indiscipline faced in an effort to get students online on time

Are among the myriads of challenges experienced by frustrated students, parents

Administrations and teachers

New strategies, new ideas

Learning how to effectively maneuver the online teaching and learning space

Planning and preparing

Ready to teach only to realize no student in plain sight

Frustrated

Virtual teaching and learning is pretty much exhausting

But at the same time very rewarding.

I don't just mean exhausting in the physical sense

Or your eyestrain sense, which is all very real

I mean exhausting in the sense that you are reimagining yourself every day

Sitting in this space, trying to figure out

How to really teach this material to students

While keeping them fully engaged

Cameras off gets very frustrating

But with careful planning with other colleagues,

Aiming to make each day's learning experience fun.

As the task of educating the nation's children

Lies predominantly in the teacher's hands.

# CELEBRATION

*A celebration is a special, enjoyable event that is organized because something pleasant has happened. It is the act or process of showing appreciation to self or someone else. Start today by celebrating you.*

# DISAPPOINTMENT LEADS TO DESTINY

Is disappointment good or bad?

Is disappointment from God?

Some will say every disappointment is for one's good.

How can this be?

Usually, the person in the situation at the time will disagree

They are not able to see any good

That will or might come out of the disappointing situation.

We have all had or have disappointment in our lives

But on the other side of every disappointment

For some of us lies destiny.

I am one such person

My destiny was on the other side of my many disappointments.

There were some things that I wanted

And clearly thought were the will of God

Over time I came to realize these were not.

In order for me to reach my destiny

God had to withhold them

And to make room for the things that would eventually lead me to

my destiny.

The process is by no means an easy one

But God continues to work his purpose out in my life

Because His aim is for me to reach my destiny

In all areas of my life.

So the truth is every disappointment is for my good

Regardless of.

I will continue to use my disappointments to get to my DESTINY

This is perfectly in line with Romans 8 v 28

Yes, all things and circumstances are always working for God's Glory

And for our good if we have faith.

Continue to press on, and your destination and your destiny will

unfold.

Once you are on the destiny path, you will eventually reach your

destination.

# UNPREDICTABLE

Life is so unpredictable

so many questions with few answers.

There are days when I am bursting with excitement that I want to

share with the world

and then there are days I just want to sit in a corner unnoticed.

There are days when my faith is as big as the universe, and then there

are days when it's smaller than a mustard seed.

There are days when I laugh so hard I cry, and then there are days I

cry so hard until it hurts.

There are days with everything matters, and there are days when

nothing matters.

There are days when everything is moving so fast

and then out of nowhere, everything stops

and it becomes as still as the sun.

There are days when I feel like all my hope is gone

and then I am reminded by His word that God is my hiding place

and my shield

I hope in your word Lord

There are days when I feel so lonely, my entire body aches

And questions of uncertainties race through my mind

And then I am reminded that God has a plan just for me

Plans to give me a hope and future

How amazing

Yet, there are times when this is so far from my human understanding

There are days when I have no words to express how I feel

While there are days when my tongue is like a pen of a skillful writer

My heart, my spirit recites your word

With my lips closed, my heart sings your praise

I was reminded today that in the stillness, God does speak.

And I should continue to listen as He speaks while embracing change.

# MY REALITY

My heart has been numb all week

As I try to piece the events that unfolded right before my very eyes

Speechless, broken, angry

Scared, frantic, pained

My emotions burst out of my heart

As I found a little strength

To muster a few words

Why Lord and why me?


Numerous thoughts and questions filled my mind

As tears flowed effortlessly from my eyes

What's happening, and is this real

We have been waiting for months.

That already felt like forever.

And now this, this cannot be

Lord, can you please answer these?

Why, when, where, how, what?

Seriously, face it, is this my reality

Food and sleep are now far from me

Windows closed, no light in sight

My heart was racing, my head aching

Eyes swollen

And the pain I feel becomes indescribable

Deep in my heart, I know I have to fight

I have been through so much in my life

And the only thing I know how to do is to call on Jesus for His help

His Word is true, and so I began speaking and declaring

Repenting if I did wrong

Searching the scriptures

Allowing it to really heal my soul

Surrendering to His will not my own

Entrusting my life in His hand

While trusting Him completely with the process

Understanding He has the answers

And it's okay if He chooses not to reveal them to me


As the days go by and turn into weeks

Another chapter has started

The pain is real

What is presented is the deal

But God reminds me daily; He still heals

And His love is unconditional and real

He is God, and He has the final say

I will continue to exercise my Faith

Knowing He is working it all out for His greatest good

I will continue to stand and declare your every word

Believing you each and every day for another miracle

This is just another test

I pledge to do my best

I will not sit still and rest

My help and strength come from Him

who is the Master of the Universe?

And while I may never know why

It's okay, Lord

I know you are awesome and mighty in all your ways

You have our best interest at heart

Align our hearts to your Word

Attune our ears to your voice

Let your Words of life roll from your lips

While we sing praises to our King

In everything, Lord, we give thee thanks.

# I SMILE

I smile because the Joy of the Lord is my strength.

I smile because God is intentional

He is working all things out for my good

I smile because I am chosen.

I smile because He knew me before I was conceived.

I smile because my steps are ordered by the Lord

I smile because I am fearfully and wonderfully made

I smile because He provides for me daily

I smile because I am alive

I smile because I am happy

I smile because I am a carrier of His Holy Spirit

I smile because I am a victor and not a victim

I smile because I am an overcomer

I smile because my test is my testimony


Truth be told, I smile not because everything is perfect

No, I smile because He makes all things perfect in His time

I smile not because all my bills are paid,

No, I smile because He promises to supply all my needs, and that

includes my bills

I smile not because I am okay,

No, I smile because I know I will be okay if I trust Him in the process

I smile not because I have great faith,

No, I smile because all I need is a mustard seed of Faith

I smile, not because I have it all figured out,

No, I smile because God has it all figured out for me

I smile because God has been so good to me,

I refuse to let anyone, or anything take away my SMILE.

And when my FACE is not SMILING, my HEART is.

# WHO IS HOLDING YOUR MIRROR ?

Who is holding your mirror?

Sometimes we allow the wrong people to hold our mirror,

What you see looking back at you

Does not accurately reflect the reality of who you are

and who God has made you to become.

The truth is there are so many things

That can smear the mirror

That will deflect or cause the image to be blurred.

Depending on the angle you are looking from

And who is looking in the mirror

Will influence what you see in that mirror.

Different people will look and see something totally different.

When you look in the mirror

And if by any chance you do not like what you see

Then you will have to decide

Do I need to change my mirrors?

Or change the image that is presented before you in the mirror.

Sometimes it is easier to change the mirror.

But would that help?

Do a self-introspect!

If the image you see in the mirror is not mirroring Christ

Then it is clear you do not need to change the mirror

You need to change the image that is presented before you in the mirror, YOU.

# DESIGN YOUR PLAN

A low place can be like a drop in a road.

When there is a dip in the terrain, the way ahead is hidden.

At such times, it is difficult to make progress.

Perhaps, "hope deferred" has made you heart-sick

and you feel as if you cannot continue.

Remember, the way out of a valley requires a climb

When you lack energy,

It is much easier to stay in a slump than to move forward.

I encourage you to get up, brush yourself and continue your journey.

# THE 8 R'S APPROACH

Restart – its ok to start over

Rebuild - from scratch

Reflect- on what went wrong and what can you change

Revisit - your goals, plans and values

Recreate- new strategies.

Reorganize- yourself, your time

Refocus- your attention on what you want to do next

Redesign -your product

Then...

Work up the courage to do it

Identify obstacles standing in your way

Design a plan to eliminate these obstacles

Overcome your fear of being wrong.

# YOU ARE GOD'S CHAMPION

When love fails and people who you put your love and trust in fail,

your life will never be the same

To suffer disappointment, loss, illness, abuse,

whether emotional, physical, financial, sexual, verbal

Trust or mistrust issues,

Loss of jobs or your own business,

Divorce, separation, death

You name it

We have all been through something

or

Continue to go through something.


These have caused pain, trauma, hurt, resentment,

Un-forgiveness, hate,

We get to that very low point in our lives

And we feel alone

What is the sense to continue?

Yes, you must continue as better days are ahead

This low place does not disqualify you from the race of life

It prepares you; it positions you

Your lowest point can become your launching pad.

The lowest place in my life became my launching pad

From writing my book, that became my success story


If you feel like you have failed to hold your ground

If you asked the question, I used to ask why me?

If your circumstances have caused you to become disheartened,

If you have been pressed on every side, misunderstood,

If you are at a frustrated point

If you feel as if what is the point, I might as well give up

I am here to encourage you and to tell you not to.


Yes, you may feel as though you are in your lowest place

And maybe, yes, you are.

But right here, the God of grace is waiting for you!

This place where you are at is where champions are birthed

You are God's Champion!!!

Do not fear mistakes but use them as stepping stones to your success. Do not be afraid to own your mistakes as you hone your skills to become not only good but great. Develop your success from your failures. There is no shame in mistakes or failures.

~Donette DaCosta

*Our desired destinations in life may not be clear and picture-perfect. Do not be afraid to own your mistakes as you hone your skills to become not only good but great regardless of the many twists and turns life throws at you. You will eventually get there.*

*~Donette DaCosta*

*He brought you here into this struggle so you could sweat out your insecurities. He brought you here into this tight place so your doubts could die and your faith could live.*

*~Donette DaCosta*

Some of the stuff you are going through is taking you to the place you asked God to take you. You just do not like how you are getting there but trust Him. Do not give up on God. He will never give up on you. He will not let you down, and neither will He leave you all by yourself. Gods got you. Trust Him in the process.

~Donette DaCosta

*All things are possible if we only believe His promises to us. Cast your cares and concern on him because He cares for you. Calm seas never made a skilled sailor.*

*~Donette DaCosta*

If you are overwhelmed right now, find peace in knowing God is big enough to meet all your needs, and He is personal enough to call every name. He did not teach you to swim to let you drown. He did not take you this far to leave you. He can handle the problems you are facing, and His hand is on your life. You are never alone.

~Donette DaCosta

www.ingramcontent.com/pod-product-compliance
Lightning Source LLC
Chambersburg PA
CBHW060835110426

R18122100001BA/R181221PG42736CBX00038BA/49